MY BIG BOOK OF

BIBLE HEROES

FOR KIDS

GLENN HASCALL

MY BIG BOOK OF
BIBLE
HEROES
FOR KIDS

Stories of 50 Weird, Wild, Wonderful People from God's Word

SHILOH kidz
An Imprint of Barbour Publishing, Inc.

© 2015 by Barbour Publishing, Inc.

Print ISBN 978-1-63409-315-6

Scripture quotations are taken from the *Holy Bible*, New Living Translation copyright© 1996, 2004, 2007 by Tyndale House Foundation. Used by permission of Tyndale House Publishers, Inc. Carol Stream, Illinois 60188. All rights reserved.

Cover and interior character illustrations: Amit Tayal

Published by Shiloh Kidz, an imprint of Barbour Publishing, Inc., P.O. Box 719, Uhrichsville, Ohio 44683, www.barbourbooks.com

Our mission is to publish and distribute inspirational products offering exceptional value and biblical encouragement to the masses.

Printed in China.
05474 0916 SC

CONTENTS

Adam: Amazed by Wonder 9

Noah: Building a Lifeboat 12

Abraham: An Altar of Trust 15

Jacob: Waiting for a Blessing 18

Joseph, Son of Jacob: Hard Times Ahead 21

Shiphrah: A Kind Choice 24

Jochebed: Rescuing a Son 27

Moses: The Reluctant Rescuer 30

Caleb: Fearless Faith 33

Joshua: Following the Leader 36

Gideon: Clay Jars and the Hand Drinkers 39

Samson: Using God's Gifts 42

Ruth: A New Family Connection 45

Hannah: Bold First Steps 48

Samuel: Doing God's Work 51

Jonathan: A Friend from the Beginning 54

Abigail: The Courage to Say "I'm Sorry" 57

David: A King Plans a Kindness 60

Nathan: Special Delivery 63

Solomon: It's Wise to Ask 66

Elijah: He Spoke the Truth 69

Elisha: "I Serve God" 72

Josiah: The Choice to Follow 75

Hezekiah: A Powerful Decision 78

Nehemiah: The Purposeful Builder 81

Esther: The Family Hero 84

Mordecai: The Right Choices 87

Job: Bad Day Survival 90

Isaiah: The Way of Promise 93

Jeremiah: Operation Obedience 96

Ezekiel: Three Special Messages 99

Daniel: Accused but Confident 102

Shadrach, Meshach, Abednego: They Stood Strong 105

Gabriel: This Is Good News 108

Mary: Ready and Willing 111

Joseph: Faithful Obedience 114

John the Baptist: Less Important 117

Jesus: A Life of Love 120

John the Disciple: A True Friend 123

James: Loyal to the End 126

Luke: Historical Friendship 129

Mary and Martha: Just a Little More Time 132

Good Samaritan: Surprised by Acceptance 135

Nicodemus: Night School 138

Simon of Cyrene: "Let Me Help You" 141

Joseph of Arimathea: An Unusual Gift 144

Peter: Forgiveness Appreciation 147

Paul: School's in Session 150

Barnabas: The Power to Encourage 153

Timothy: He Chose to Follow 156

INTRODUCTION

You're probably already familiar with many fictional superheroes—Batman, Spider-Man, Superman. . .the list goes on and on! Now meet some of the real men and women of the Bible whose lives provided positive examples centuries before the printing of the first comic book.

God's Big Book (the Bible) is filled with stories. Some are happy. Some are sad. Some filled with bad guys. Some filled with heroes. All good stories have heroes, and every hero must overcome a great difficulty. After all, you can't become heroic if life is always easy. The hard times these heroes faced made them outstanding role models.

This book is all about the heroes. These heroes weren't perfect, they didn't always make the right choices, and they sometimes questioned what God asked them to do. But they were heroes because they trusted God despite everything and continued to believe His promises.

So let's take some time and read these stories. Discover the heroes with traits such as obedience, trust, patience, determination, mercy, and love. At the end of each story spend some time thinking about the strengths these heroes show. You'll find some ideas and questions to help you personalize and adopt the traits of a hero into your own life.

Some stories may be familiar and some may be less known, but fifty weird, wild, and wonderful heroes await you in the pages of this book!

ADAM

Story Address:
Genesis 2–3

Heroic Quality:
Wonder

Be Heroic:
*Future generations will hear
about the wonders of the Lord.*
PSALM 22:30

Amazed by Wonder

The world was new. The animals needed names. Adam had a job to do.

God created the animals so Adam could find a friend, but each animal was different. The elephant was nothing like the wolf. The owl was nothing like the hummingbird. The shark was nothing like the clown fish. Adam had to recognize the differences and then name each animal.

Adam was filled with wonder at the beauty of the leopard, the strength of the ox, and the grace of the eagle.

He took pleasure in trees covered in leaves, flowers in bloom, and rivers clear enough to see each fish. God had created this paradise for Adam to enjoy.

Each day was an adventure. He could explore. He could run. He could laugh.

He was alone.

The wonder was amazing, but something was missing. Soon the naming of the animals would be done. Someday he would have explored every part of the garden. Some days he wondered why there was no one just like him to share the wonder. Sometimes he talked to the animals, but they didn't understand.

Then God made a new decision. God would make Adam sleep, and when he woke up, he would no longer be alone.

When Adam opened his eyes he saw someone who was like him, but not entirely. He saw someone who smiled, laughed, and understood. Her name was Eve. She was the "just right" answer to his loneliness. She was his helper, companion, and friend. She was a wonder.

"Finally," Adam said. "Eve is a part of me. She is like me. I am no longer alone."

Each day Adam found new marvels and shared them with Eve. Sometimes Eve would discover extraordinary things and show Adam.

If wonder for God's creation made Adam a hero, then disobedience made him forget.

God told the first man and woman not to eat from a certain tree He had made. It was the only rule the couple had to follow. When Adam stopped seeing the wonder in every caterpillar, butterfly, and bumblebee, he had time to think about the tree God didn't want him to think about.

Eve was thinking about the tree, too. She was the first to eat, and she convinced Adam to eat the fruit as well.

Suddenly Adam had less interest in the wonder of animals, plants, and fish. He was less amazed at the beauty of the first garden. He struggled to enjoy what he saw because he knew how he felt, which was awful.

He and Eve hid from God. They were ashamed. They were sad. They felt alone.

The man and woman learned that disobedience makes wonder less wonderful. The beautiful things that usually took Adam and Eve's breath away seemed unimportant after they disobeyed.

God told Adam, "The ground is now diseased. Where beautiful flowers once grew, you will find thorns. You will have to work hard to grow food to eat. You will grow old and die."

Then Adam and Eve left the beautiful garden at God's command.

Adam was the first to show wonder at all the beauty that God had created. His first days of friendship with God were pure, and God was pleased with Adam. When Adam and Eve sinned, everything changed. Beauty still existed in the world, but not like it had. The good news is the heroic character of wonder still shows up in all who fully obey God's commands. When you obey, you'll always find those things God calls beautiful.

LEARNING FROM A HERO

God created a perfect world. Adam was impressed. We can learn a lot from Adam's wonder.

1. If you were Adam, what would fill you with wonder?
2. What makes new experiences wonderful?
3. How can you find wonder in ordinary things?

Wonder is a choice to look at everything the way God does. He created this world for us to enjoy.

NOAH

Story Address:
Genesis 6–9

Heroic Quality:
Obedient

Be Heroic:
"If you love me,
obey my commandments."
John 14:15

Building a Lifeboat

God looked at the people who lived on earth. They were mean. They were cruel. They would not follow Him.

The only family in the world who listened to God was Noah's family. God liked Noah.

One day God said to Noah, "The people have become violent and cruel. They do not follow Me. I am starting over."

Noah listened carefully as God continued, "I want you to build a very large boat." Then God told Noah how long, high, and wide to make the boat. He told him what wood to use and how to make it so it wouldn't leak. He told him to build three decks inside the boat. Then God shared His plan with Noah. "I will soon cover the entire earth with a flood. Everything that is not on the boat will be destroyed with water. I want you to take your family into the boat along with a pair of each kind of animal. This is My way of making sure there will be new animals when the flood is over. You won't need to worry about finding the animals, because I will bring them to you. Make sure you have enough food to feed yourself and all the animals."

Noah and his three sons, Shem, Ham, and Japheth, started building the boat that God would use to save those who believed enough to get on the boat. The boat was very big, so it took many years to build.

One day God said to Noah, "It's time to get on the boat. Take your wife, your sons, and their wives. You are the only righteous people left on earth. In one week the rains will come and will fall for forty days. The earth will be covered."

When all the animals and all of Noah's family were on the ark, God shut the door.

On the seventh day, Noah heard the rain. Soon the boat began to float. Day after day the rain fell. Noah's sons fed the animals. God had promised to make all things new, and He was keeping His promise.

For many months Noah and his family lived inside the big boat.

The day came when the boat landed on a mountain. Noah's family and all the animals had to wait until the water went down enough for them to be safe walking on the ground again.

When they finally came out of the ark, there were no animals and no cities. They didn't recognize anything.

Noah and his family worshipped God.

The family looked in the sky and saw a rainbow. This was the symbol of God's promise never to destroy the earth with a flood again. God said, "People will always make wrong choices. They will disobey Me.

They will sin. But I will never destroy all living things again. I will make sure there will be every season, night and day, and that the ground will produce food."

When the animals were released from Noah's big boat, they found new homes and new animals were born. The wives of Noah's sons also had children.

Noah was chosen to build the boat because he was righteous. Noah showed he loved God by obeying Him. Most people thought building a boat on dry ground was a bad idea, but Noah understood that God wanted him to obey, so he fully obeyed.

Sometimes we don't think it's important to obey God. Noah's big boat showed that God has always wanted us to obey, and when He says He will do something, we can believe He will.

LEARNING FROM A HERO

God asked Noah to do something that seemed strange. God knew He could trust Noah when Noah chose to obey.

1. Why is it hard to obey the first time you're told?
2. How did Noah show that he could obey God?
3. What do you think would have happened if Noah had not fully obeyed?

When we obey, we agree that God's rules are worth following.

ABRAHAM

Story Address:
Genesis 22

Heroic Quality:
Trust

Be Heroic:
I trust in God, so why should I be afraid?
Psalm 56:4

An Altar of Trust

It was a beautiful morning, but Abraham didn't notice. God had spoken to Abraham the day before and asked him to do something that made no sense, but he could not refuse.

"Come, my son," Abraham said to his son Isaac, "we have a long journey, and you must join me."

"A journey?" Isaac said happily. He loved spending time with his father, and this day seemed the start of a great adventure. "You chopped wood already?"

"Yes," Abraham said quietly. "There will be a sacrifice."

Two servants followed the father and son.

The trip was long. For two nights they slept under the stars, and Isaac listened to the servants tell stories of their youth. Abraham said very little.

On the third morning, Abraham looked into the distance and said, "Isaac and I will go on alone. Stay here and wait."

The servants stopped as Abraham placed the burden of chopped wood on Isaac's back.

The father and son walked quietly toward a mountain. The older man was unwilling to speak, and the young man was unsure why his father was so quiet.

Then Isaac remembered something his father had said when they started this journey. "Father?" he asked.

"Yes, my son," Abraham sighed.

"I'm carrying the wood, and you carry the torch, but I don't see a sacrifice for the offering."

"God will provide," was all his father would say.

As Isaac walked, he thought of home, friends, and what his future would be like. He might have been happy with these thoughts, but he felt his father's sadness with every step he took.

Suddenly Abraham stopped and gathered stones to make an altar. Isaac found rocks his dad could use. Once the altar was built, Abraham remembered what God had said: "Take your son Isaac, whom you love so much, and go to the land of Moriah. Go and sacrifice him as a burnt offering."

God had always been trustworthy. God's way had always been right. God's gifts were always good.

Had Abraham heard God right?

On that day on Mount Moriah, Abraham trusted that God knew what He was doing.

Isaac was called the son of promise. God had said that Isaac would have many children and grandchildren. His family would become great. Abraham didn't know how God could keep His promise, but he continued to trust.

When the young man understood that he was to be the sacrifice, he was confused, but he, too, trusted his father. Up on the altar Isaac went. What would happen now?

Suddenly Abraham heard a voice say, "Do not hurt your son in any way. You love God, and you were willing to follow His command. You were willing to give the thing you loved most to God." This was the voice of one of God's angels.

Abraham gladly helped his son down from the altar. He hugged him and found it hard to speak.

Then they heard a noise. A ram had caught his horns in a nearby bush.

God had provided the sacrifice.

Abraham may not have understood everything about God's command, but God had always been trustworthy, so Abraham trusted God.

Maybe God was showing each of us what a difficult thing it would be to sacrifice a son. Yet this is exactly what God did when Jesus came to earth to pay for the sin of everyone. God provided a sacrifice for Abraham that day. God provided a sacrifice for each us of—Jesus. God can be trusted.

LEARNING FROM A HERO

Abraham trusted God. He didn't beg God to change His mind but instead believed God's promise.

1. Why is it hard to trust people?
2. How did Abraham's story change the way you think about trust?
3. How has God shown you that He is trustworthy?

We all struggle with trust. When people don't keep their promises, it's hard to be a trust hero. When God makes a promise, He'll keep it.

JACOB

Story Address:
Genesis 32

Heroic Quality:
Determination

Be Heroic:
Jacob said, "I will not let you
go unless you bless me."
GENESIS 32:26

Waiting for a Blessing

Jacob had a problem making good choices. He liked to trick people. Once he tricked his twin brother, Esau, into selling his birthright for a pot of stew. Sure, Esau was hungry, but selling the right to be considered the firstborn son was a high price for something to eat.

When the twins' dad, Isaac, was dying, he asked Esau to go hunting and make him a good meal. Once he had eaten the meal, he promised to bless Esau. What did Jacob do? He wore some of Esau's clothes, made some food, and pretended to be Esau. His father was surprised at how fast the meal was prepared, but his eyes were weak and he couldn't see that the food was not from Esau. The father ate the tasty meal and then blessed Jacob instead of Esau.

Yes, Jacob was tricky, and it got him into trouble with his brother. After Isaac died, Jacob left home because he was worried about what Esau might do to him.

If you thought Jacob was tricky, you should read about his uncle Laban. Jacob went to work for his uncle so he could marry Laban's daughter Rachel. The agreement was that Jacob would work seven years, and then he could get married. So Jacob worked hard, but when the wedding day arrived, Laban tricked Jacob and he actually married Rachel's older sister.

Laban told Jacob that instead of money he would give him animals from the flocks. Laban always tried to give him animals nobody would want. Then he kept changing the agreement. Jacob was learning that it was no fun to be tricked.

During those hard years, Jacob finally grew up. He had been an adult for a long time, but he needed to learn responsibility and how important it is to ask for forgiveness.

After he took his family away from Laban's farm, he had to ask his brother, Esau, to forgive him. He was a better example to his children. He had a meeting with God.

One night when Jacob was near the Jabbok River, he sent his family to the other side while he stayed in a camp he had made.

In the darkness someone came into Jacob's camp. The two began to wrestle, and Jacob realized this was not a man. During the struggle Jacob's hip was injured, but he held on tightly. When the morning came, the one he fought said, "You must let me go."

Jacob gasped and said, "Not until you bless me."

"What is your name?" he was asked.

"Jacob," came the reply.

"Not anymore. You have a new name. You will be known as Israel because you have fought with God and man."

Then the wrestling match was over. Jacob's determination changed him. He limped for the rest of his life, but God had given him a new name. His future showed the change. His brother forgave him. God gave him a large family. Jacob honored God at last.

To be determined to follow God means you have decided to cooperate with His plan for you. Because God said you shouldn't steal, you cooperate by not stealing. Because God said to honor Him above everything, you honor God above all. You will make mistakes, but to be determined means you really want to love God by doing the things He commands. And when you fail, you must admit your mistake and accept forgiveness.

Jacob did not cooperate for a long time. He used tricks to get what he wanted. God wanted Jacob to trust Him enough to let Him help.

LEARNING FROM A HERO

God knows how to get our attention so we can see the importance of following Him.

1. Does God want you to be honest or tricky?
2. Why don't you like to be around people who trick you?
3. How can you cooperate with God today?

It's good to know that even when we make wrong choices God doesn't give up on us. Determine to do what God asks.

JOSEPH
SON OF JACOB

Story Address:
Genesis 37, 39–41

Heroic Quality:
Endurance

Be Heroic:
*Patient endurance is
what you need now.*
Hebrews 10:36

Hard Times Ahead

Joseph was the favorite son of Jacob. His ten older brothers didn't like Joseph very much.

Joseph watched his father's sheep. Every time he visited his brothers, Joseph told his father all the bad things they were doing.

Jacob gave Joseph a very colorful robe because he loved him so much. This made the brothers even unhappier with Joseph.

Joseph was young and didn't realize how his words made his brothers feel.

One day his brothers were working out in the country. Joseph's father wanted to know how things were going, so Joseph went to see them. The brothers did not want to see him. In fact, they were so angry they were ready to kill their young brother. Instead, they put him in a well. They grabbed his special robe and ripped it. They planned to lie to their dad. They would tell him that a wild animal had killed Joseph and show him the ripped robe.

Joseph's brother Reuben wanted to rescue Joseph from the well, but the other brothers saw some men on a nearby road. These men bought and sold slaves. The brothers sold Joseph to the men.

For years the brothers lied to their father about what happened to Joseph. Jacob spent many years thinking Joseph was dead.

Meanwhile, Joseph was taken to Egypt and sold to an Egyptian soldier named Potiphar.

Joseph had to grow up very fast. He wasn't a favorite son in Egypt. He was a slave. He had to work hard. He had to put up with hard days.

His brothers lied about what happened to Joseph. Potiphar's wife lied about him, too.

Potiphar didn't ask Joseph what happened. He just threw him in jail.

Joseph had to start from the beginning. No special coat. No encouraging words from his father. He went from being a slave to being a prisoner.

Joseph endured his time in the prison. God had a plan for Joseph, and the young man was in training. The warden was impressed with Joseph and put him in charge of the entire prison.

God also helped Joseph understand dreams. This was a big part of God's plan.

One night Pharaoh had a dream he didn't understand. No one could interpret what it meant. Someone who had been in prison with Joseph remembered that he could understand dreams and told Pharaoh.

After so many years in prison, Joseph was going to meet Pharaoh. God helped Joseph understand the dream. There would be seven years when crops would not grow. If no one planned for this, then there would not be enough food to eat.

Pharaoh was so impressed he made Joseph the second most important ruler in Egypt. Joseph had endured so much, and now he would help the country endure the bad years ahead.

Joseph had grown up. He had forgiven his brothers. He had prepared for the famine.

One day his brothers came to Egypt to buy food. They didn't recognize Joseph. It wasn't long before Jacob learned that Joseph was alive. It wasn't long before Joseph saw all his family. It wasn't long before Pharaoh gave Joseph a place where his family could live nearby.

Joseph endured hard times, and God used those difficult times to help save Egypt—and to help save Joseph's family.

Sometimes God uses hard things to make us more like the people He always wanted us to be. God wants us to endure. When we stand strong in difficult situations, we will learn more about the faithfulness of the God who has always had a plan for us.

LEARNING FROM A HERO

Joseph had a hard life. When Joseph endured bad days, God used what he learned to save Joseph's family.

1. Why would it have been easy for Joseph to give up?
2. How can God use endurance to help you?
3. Can you name ways you've endured hard days?

God wants us to help people who struggle, but He also wants us to know He can help us learn important things when we endure, just like Joseph did.

SHIPHRAH

Story Address:
Exodus 1:15–22

Heroic Quality:
Mercy

Be Heroic:
"God blesses those who are merciful."
Matthew 5:7

A Kind Choice

Every day Shiphrah was busy helping deliver babies. She was called a midwife. She knew what to do to help new moms. She was good at her job. Shiphrah loved babies.

God had given her the skill to do her job well, but she would become a hero of mercy.

She had watched many of the children she saw as babies grow into strong men and women. She loved this part of her job the most. God was making sure the family of Abraham grew larger every day. Shiphrah had been chosen to help. She was very busy.

The king of Egypt was not happy to see the family of Abraham growing so big. Too many baby boys might mean there would be too many strong men in the future. Maybe they would fight against him. Maybe they would refuse to be slaves anymore. Something had to be done.

The family of Abraham lived in Egypt at that time, but it was not their home. The Egyptian king made them slaves even though God once used their relative Joseph to save Egypt during a time when it was so dry nothing would grow. Egypt might not have survived without God using Joseph to help the pharaoh know what he should do.

The king told Shiphrah and the other midwives, "I know you help the women in Abraham's family give birth. You are there when their babies are born. You are the perfect people to help me with my new rule. These are the instructions you must follow. All baby girls will be allowed to live, but you must kill all the baby boys."

Shiphrah loved God. She obeyed God. She did not follow the king's evil rule.

The king had expected to hear how sad the people in Abraham's family were when there were no baby boys, but he did not hear any sadness or see them upset. He expected fewer people, but Abraham's family continued to grow. He saw baby boys among Abraham's family. Why hadn't Shiphrah and the other midwives killed the baby boys? The king was angry.

But God was pleased with Shiphrah and the other midwives, for they had shown mercy to the baby boys.

Shiphrah's mercy allowed Moses to be born. Moses would be used by God to lead Abraham's family out of Egypt to a new land He would give them.

God honored Shiphrah by giving her a family of her own. Her mercy had been rewarded. Soon the people would leave Egypt and the king's wicked rule.

God wants us to show others what mercy looks like. Mercy is refusing to punish someone for something they've done even when you could. Shiphrah was told by the king to kill baby boys. Shiphrah was merciful and allowed the baby boys to live.

We are merciful when we forgive others. We are merciful when we love people who may be hard to love. We are merciful when we are kind to people who don't deserve it.

God has always been merciful. He has always loved us. He is willing to forgive us.

Mercy does what no one expects but everyone secretly hopes for. Mercy is just one way we can show love to other people. It's one way to show that God cares. It is something everyone needs. It is something you can give. Be a hero. Show mercy.

LEARNING FROM A HERO

Shiphrah knew God was kind. She made the decision to show that kind mercy to others.

1. Would it be easier to obey God or the king?
2. Why is mercy something all of us need?
3. How can you show mercy to others?

We should be kind because God is kind. We show mercy because God has forgiven us.

JOCHEBED

Story Address:
Exodus 1–6

Heroic Quality:
Respect

Be Heroic:
"You must not murder."
Exodus 20:13

Rescuing a Son

The king of Egypt was frightened. It had been many years since the relatives of Abraham came to live in Egypt. Now there were so many of them that he thought they might become strong enough to take away his kingdom.

The king made a very bad rule. He said that anyone who helped a Hebrew woman when she was giving birth was to kill the baby if the baby was a boy. But the Hebrew midwives feared God more than they feared the king, and they refused to kill the baby boys.

The king made another very bad rule when he learned that the baby boys were still alive. He said that any boy born into Abraham's family must be thrown into the Nile River.

Jochebed and her husband, Amram, had three children. The oldest were Aaron and Miriam. Miriam didn't have to worry about the bad rule because she was a girl. Aaron didn't need to worry about the king's bad rule because he was not a baby. The bad rule meant that if anyone found baby Moses, he could be killed. This made his family very sad.

Jochebed knew that God respected life. So she respected the life of her baby son.

The mother hid her son for three months. Maybe she thought the king would change his mind about the very bad rule. Soon baby Moses was too big to hide.

The family thought about all the ways they could try to save the youngest member of their family. In the end they made a floating basket for Moses. The baby's sister, Miriam, watched as the basket floated gently on the ripples of the Nile River near some reeds.

Soon the royal princess came down to the water. Miriam was frightened. The only thing Moses' older sister could do was watch as the princess saw the floating basket. The princess asked someone to wade into the water to see what it was. The basket was gently pulled to shore.

The princess opened the basket to see a baby boy blinking in the sunlight. When Moses began to cry, Miriam stopped hiding. She ran to the princess and said, "Would you like me to find someone from Abraham's family to help take care of him?"

The princess thought this was a very good idea. The princess did not know that Jochebed, the baby's real mother, would be the one to help care for her own son.

Jochebed stood before the princess, looking at her son. The princess said, "Please take care of him for me. If you will help me, I will pay you."

When Moses was older, he left his father, mother, sister, and brother to live in the palace. The princess had adopted the young relative of

Abraham. When Moses grew up, God used him to rescue His people from slavery.

The king wanted all babies, including Moses, to die because he was frightened by how strong the Hebrew people were becoming. God rescued Moses and made him part of the Egyptian king's family.

Jochebed respected life and trusted God. God honored her for it.

God wants us to respect life. That means we show honor to people who are older than us. We show kindness to people who are younger than us. We love people no matter where they come from or what family they belong to.

God created everyone, and He wants us to respect others. We don't even have to agree with everything they do to love them the way God wants us to.

LEARNING FROM A HERO

Jochebed was a hero. She respected life, and God was pleased.

1. What makes it hard to show love to people who are different?
2. Why do you think God tells us to love others?
3. How can you show respect to your own family?

Jochebed wanted to save her son. God helped her. God can help you respect life.

MOSES

Story Address:
Exodus 2—20

Heroic Quality:
Leadership

Be Heroic:
*Without wise leadership,
a nation falls.*
Proverbs 11:14

The Reluctant Rescuer

Moses was the adopted son of an Egyptian princess, but he was also the birth son of a Hebrew slave woman.

As a man he left Egypt and lived in the wilderness for many years. He married, had children, and lived far away from Egypt.

Moses was watching his flocks one day when he saw a small bush. It was burning, but it didn't burn up. It just kept burning.

Suddenly a voice said, "Moses!"

"I am here," said Moses in awe.

"I am Abraham's God," said the voice, "and the ground you are standing on is holy. Take off your sandals."

Moses was afraid. He removed his sandals, and God spoke once more: "My people are slaves in Egypt. They are suffering. Their cries for help have reached me in heaven. I have come to rescue them. I am sending you to lead them into a land where they will be free. It is a land that grows good vegetables and fruit. Go to Pharaoh. You have a big job. I will go with you. Look around you. What do you see?"

Moses looked past the burning bush. "I see a mountain."

God said, "When you lead the people out of Egypt, you will return to this mountain and you will worship Me here."

Moses was not sure about his new job.

"Pharaoh will be stubborn," God said. "He will not let the people leave until I force him to let them go. Expect ten miracles. After the last miracle, the people will give you gifts and Pharaoh will insist that you leave."

Moses was uncomfortable. "I am not the right man for the job. I can't say the right words. When I want to say something important, the wrong words come out."

God was firm. "Who made the mouth? Who gave speech? I did. I will go with you. I will tell you what to say."

Moses stood before Pharaoh, and ten plagues came to Egypt. Each plague was worse than the one before. Moses turned water into blood, then frogs covered the land, followed by lice, flies, sick livestock, boils, hail, locusts, darkness, and the death of the firstborn sons. God protected His people from each plague.

On the night of the last plague, God told the Hebrews to make special food. This would be the first of the annual memory meals known as Passover. The people needed to remember how God saved them, so this story would be one that is shared to this day.

Moses became a great leader. He followed God's orders, and the people walked on dry land through the great Red Sea. The people were hungry, and when Moses prayed, God sent a sweet food called manna that they could gather every day. When the people needed water, Moses prayed and God provided.

God gave Moses the Ten Commandments. God gave Moses a cloud to follow when the sun was up and a pillar of fire to follow when the sun was down.

Even though the people grumbled sometimes, they followed Moses and they worshipped at the mountain just as God promised.

God doesn't always choose people who think they are ready to be leaders. Many times God picks someone who will follow Him, and then He teaches him or her to lead.

Moses never thought he was the right man to lead. In fact, he thought he was the last person anyone should look to as a leader. God knew Moses better than Moses knew himself. Moses was just the right leader at just the right time.

LEARNING FROM A HERO

Even when Moses was reluctant, he was a hero for the people of Israel who cried out to God for help.

1. Why do you think Moses argued with God?
2. Can you tell about a time when you needed God to help you?
3. Why is it important to remember that God is always the One to help?

God's best leaders are people who are willing to follow.

CALEB

Heroic Quality:
Fearless

Be Heroic:
[Caleb said,] "I wholeheartedly followed the LORD my God."
JOSHUA 14:8

Fearless Faith

Caleb waited to see who would be chosen to explore Canaan. God had promised a new home for the large number of people who had left Egypt. Then Caleb heard his name.

Perhaps they meant another Caleb. But Moses called out, "Caleb, son of Jephunneh of the family of Judah."

He had been chosen to explore. He stood with eleven other men who would travel to Canaan to learn what they could about the land God said was theirs.

For forty days the men explored a land filled with all kinds of fruit and crops. Two of the men cut down a cluster of grapes. It took both men to carry the fruit.

"This land is perfect for our families," Caleb laughed.

"I think so, too," said Joshua.

They looked over the cities, the farmland, the hills, and the rivers. There was more than enough land and food to take care of every family.

Caleb was ready to move in, but they still had to tell Moses what they saw. Caleb was certain that when the people heard what the land was like, they would be ready to accept God's gift.

The people cheered when Caleb and the rest of the adventurers came back from Canaan. They were amazed at the size of the cluster of grapes. Who had ever seen any this large?

Moses said, "Please tell us what you saw."

One of the adventurers stood up and said, "We spent more than a month exploring this new land. This is what it is like to grow anything in Canaan." He pointed to the grapes.

The people seemed pleased, amazed, and ready to start their new lives. Imagine how surprised Caleb was when the man continued. "However, the people who live there are strong, and we even saw giants. We were brick makers in Egypt. How can we win against giants?"

Caleb could see that the people were afraid. He stood up quickly and said, "God is with us. We should go right now and take the land He promised us." The people did not believe they could. Caleb continued, "This land is ours. God has given it to us. We should not wait."

"We were like grasshoppers compared to the size of the men living there," said another explorer. The people became afraid of God's gift. Caleb wondered how that was possible.

The next day the people said they should have stayed in Egypt because they would die in the wilderness without a home. Some were ready for a new leader to take them back to Egypt.

Caleb tried to quiet the crowd. "The land is wonderful," he said. "If we have pleased God, He will give us this rich land. If the Lord is with us, we never need to be afraid."

Fear was stronger than faith that day. God was not pleased. He said that if the people would not take the land He had given them, then they would stay in the wilderness one year for every day Caleb, Joshua, and the others explored the land. For forty years the people had no home because they refused to accept God's gift.

Caleb was fearless. He wanted to move into Canaan when he first saw it, and when he was an old man and the people finally came to claim this land, he was quick to ask for a place he could finally call home.

When you do what God asks, you have no reason to be afraid.

LEARNING FROM A HERO

Caleb knew he had no reason to be afraid because God always does what He says He will do.

1. What things make you afraid?
2. Why was it easy for Caleb to believe God could do what He said?
3. How can learning more about God make you less afraid?

You'll always find fear when you fail to trust God. Trusting God makes fear an unwelcome visitor.

JOSHUA

Story Address:
Joshua 6, 24

Heroic Quality:
Faithful

Be Heroic:
[God] protects those who
are faithful to him.
PROVERBS 2:8

Following the Leader

Joshua had been a slave in Egypt with the rest of his family. When God sent Moses to free the Hebrew slaves, Joshua watched as frogs, flies, and locusts covered the land. Pharaoh didn't want to let the people go, but God rescued His people.

God chose Joshua to lead the former Hebrew slaves into their own country after spending forty years in the wilderness. He had seen miracle after miracle, and he obeyed God.

Because Joshua was the new leader, he wanted to know what he should do. He asked and God answered. "Joshua, you can count on Me. Every step you take I will walk with you. Every enemy you face I will face," God said. "Be strong. Fill yourself with courage. I promised a home for your families, and I will give it to you. I will not leave you. But Joshua, you will need to know My instructions. You must obey Me in everything you do. Don't put words in My mouth. What I have said is what I mean. Think often of my words. You will be successful if you follow Me."

The way God does things is very different from the way we do things. What is hard for us is easy for Him. For Joshua, the battle of Jericho was one of those different kind of things.

God told Joshua the city was going to be given to his family. The city had high walls, and the people who lived inside could fight.

God spoke to Joshua again: "For six days you should walk around Jericho once a day. Take seven priests and your warriors. The priests should blow their horns. On the seventh day the priests and warriors should walk around the city seven times. Then the priests should play their horns loudly and all the people should yell."

That may have sounded strange to Joshua, but he was faithful to follow God's instructions. Each day the men marched and the horns played. Each day the people of Jericho looked down from their walls wondering what Joshua was doing. On the seventh day, the march didn't stop with one trip around the city. When the priests and the warriors finished walking seven times around the city, the noise of marching and horns stopped. Then the priests blew their horns with all their might. All the people shouted. While they were shouting, the high walls began to crack, the earth began to tremble, and the walls fell down.

It's easy to believe God can be trusted when you see miracles. It's harder when you don't.

In the years after God helped Joshua win the battle of Jericho, the people who had seen God break down the walls of the city stopped following God's instructions. They thought the rules were made for other people.

Joshua was sad. Joshua was disappointed. He said, "Some of you have stopped serving God. Now is the time to make a choice. There are plenty of idols of wood and metal you could serve, or you could serve God. My family has already decided. We will only serve God."

Then the people remembered who had rescued them so many times. They remembered how God had given them everything they needed in the wilderness. They remembered Jericho. That's when they said, "We, too, will follow God."

God is always looking for faithful people who will follow His instructions.

LEARNING FROM A HERO

Joshua had seen how faithful God had been. Joshua wanted to be faithful to God.

1. If you could have been at Jericho when the walls came down, how do you think you would have felt?
2. How did God show He was faithful?
3. How did Joshua show he was faithful?

We show God that we are faithful when we follow His instructions and trust in His ability to care for us.

GIDEON

Story Address:
Judges 7

Heroic Quality:
Soldier

Be Heroic:
O LORD, I give my life to you.
PSALM 25:1

Clay Jars and the Hand Drinkers

Gideon was a judge. When Gideon was alive, there was no king in Israel, so the people looked to the judges to help them make decisions. The judges asked God for help.

The people of Midian were mean to the people of Israel for seven years. God said it was time for a change, and He wanted Gideon to be a leader in making them stop. God had called Gideon a mighty soldier, but Gideon didn't always feel like a hero.

When people found out that God was going to help stop Midian, they came to meet Gideon. More than 32,000 men covered the hills around the judge. If this was going to be a battle, then the men wanted Gideon to know they would fight.

Gideon tried to quiet the men. He said, "I know some of you are afraid. Midian has been mean for a long time. You may not believe you can fight against them. If you feel timid about fighting, you should return to your homes."

At first no one moved, but as Gideon continued to look over the crowd, he saw small groups of men beginning to leave. Soon larger groups left. Once all those who were frightened had gone, only 10,000 soldiers were left.

Then God told Gideon something that seemed very strange, "You still have too many. I can rescue with many or with few, but I will rescue."

Gideon was told to take the soldiers to the river to get a drink. He was supposed to pay attention to who drank water from their hands and who drank water directly from the river.

He put the men in two groups. The "river drinkers" had more than 9,000 men. The "hand drinkers" had only 300. God said, "I will rescue Israel with 300 men. Send the others home."

Gideon must have been concerned. Midian had many soldiers. Those soldiers had a lot of training. He had only 300 men who were chosen simply because they drank water from their hands. How could God save his country using men who were not trained soldiers? How could his country be rescued from so many by so few?

God wanted Gideon to be encouraged. He told him to hide near the Midianite camp at night. All the soldiers were staying there. As he listened he heard two men talking.

"I had a strange dream last night," said the first.

"A dream?" asked the second.

"You wouldn't like this one," said the first. "A large loaf of bread rolled into our camp. It was so big it knocked down our tent."

The second thought for a minute and then said fearfully, "I know what your dream means—God has given Gideon victory over Midian."

Both men were afraid.

Gideon returned to his 300 soldiers in the darkness and handed out some very unusual weapons. They were given clay jars and horns to blow.

The soldiers were divided into three groups, and they surrounded the camp of Midian. When Gideon walked close to the camp, the soldiers all broke their clay jars, and those who had horns blew them as hard as they could. Then all the men shouted, "For the Lord and for Gideon!"

The Midianite soldiers were so confused and fearful they started fighting each other. They all panicked and ran away. Gideon and 300 soldiers watched as God did something amazing.

Three hundred men could not take the credit. They had not even fought in that battle. They obeyed God, and He deserved the credit.

LEARNING FROM A HERO

Soldiers obey God's commands. Gideon gave 300 soldiers a chance to see God do a miracle.

1. How did fewer soldiers win a fight against a large army?
2. Why is it hard to think God can use you?
3. When can God be trusted to help in hard times?

God doesn't need us to be the best at something in order to use us to do something wonderful.

SAMSON

Story Address:
Judges 13–16

Heroic Quality:
Strength

Be Heroic:
The LORD is my strength and shield.
PSALM 28:7

Using God's Gifts

Samson was the strongest man anyone had ever seen. When he was born he was dedicated to God. One of the rules he had to follow was that he would never cut his hair. By obeying God in this way, he would stay strong.

The Philistines were always looking for ways to hurt Abraham's family. Samson wanted to protect his family. He used his strength to lift the heavy gates from a Philistine city and carry them far away. Samson also burned some of the Philistine crops. The Philistines did not like Samson.

They looked for ways to capture Samson, but he was so strong he always got away.

Samson met a woman named Delilah. He thought he loved her. Delilah didn't love Samson. She was friends with the Philistines.

When the Philistines found out Samson really liked her, they came to Delilah and said, "Trick Samson into telling you what makes him so strong. We want to capture Samson, but he is too strong. If you find out how to make him weak, each of us will give you more money than you need."

Samson liked talking to Delilah. One day she asked, "Be honest. What makes you so strong? How could someone capture you?"

Samson realized she was trying to trick him, so he said, "You know the men who make the bows and arrows for hunting? If you were to get seven new strings they use to make the bows and tie me up, then I would be as weak as anyone."

Delilah believed him. When Samson fell asleep, she tied him up in the thick string, but when he woke up, he broke the string as if it were thread.

Delilah tried again, and Samson told her new ropes would make him weak, but they didn't.

Delilah tried a third time, and Samson told her that if she wove his hair into a machine that made fabric, he would become weak, but that didn't work either.

"Samson, you tell me you love me, but you won't share your secret with me." Delilah pouted. "You have made fun of me three times. Why won't you tell me the truth?"

One day Samson looked at Delilah and grew quiet. Delilah knew this was important. "No one has ever cut my hair," he began. "I was dedicated to God when I was born. The secret to my strength is obeying God. I cannot cut my hair. If that happened I really would become weak."

Now Delilah was quiet. She knew Samson had finally told her the truth.

She called the Philistine leaders and told them all she had learned. Then, while Samson slept, the Philistines shaved his head. Samson's strength was gone.

Delilah said, "The enemy is here."

Samson rose up, but something was wrong. God was not with him anymore.

The Philistines captured Samson. His new job was pushing a large grinding stone. He had disobeyed God, but each day his hair grew longer. God was once again with Samson. Samson's final act of strength was in the Philistine temple where they did not worship God. Samson stood between two pillars. He pushed against them with his hands, and the building was destroyed.

God can use our strengths to do big things. You can be a singer, artist, or athlete. Honor God with your strengths.

LEARNING FROM A HERO

Samson wasn't strong just because he had long hair. God gave him strength when he obeyed.

1. How did Samson obey God?
2. Why was it a bad idea to listen to Delilah?
3. How can you be strong for God?

Strength is something God can use when we agree to use it to honor Him.

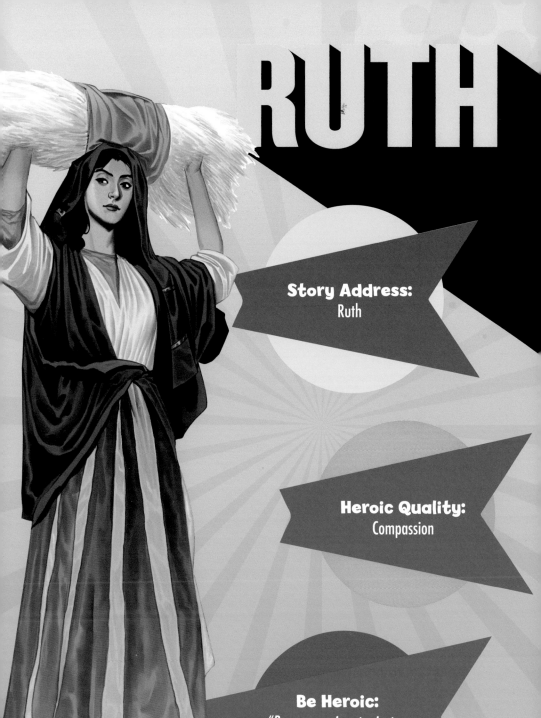

RUTH

Story Address:
Ruth

Heroic Quality:
Compassion

Be Heroic:
"Be compassionate, just as
[God] is compassionate."
LUKE 6:36

A New Family Connection

Crops wouldn't grow in Bethlehem. The sun was too hot. The soil was too dry. The ground was too hard.

Elimelech and his family moved away to the land of Moab. If they thought things were bad in Bethlehem, they were even worse in Moab. Elimelech soon grew sick and died. After his two sons were married, they also died.

This left Elimelech's wife, Naomi, and her daughters-in-law, Ruth and Orpah. It had been many years since Naomi left Bethlehem. Maybe things were better in her homeland.

Naomi decided to leave Moab and return to her family in Bethlehem. She was surprised when Ruth told her she wanted to come with her. Naomi told Ruth she should stay with her own family, but Ruth said, "Please don't ask me to leave. I will go where you go. I will live wherever you live. I will accept your family as my family. I will worship your God. Please, take me with you."

Naomi couldn't stay in Moab, and Ruth wouldn't let her go alone. The two women started their long journey. When they were close, they could see that the crops had grown again. The people were in the fields harvesting barley.

This was good news. When people didn't have much money, they were welcome to look through fields that were already harvested. Anything they found they could keep. Ruth went out every day and came home with food that she and Naomi could eat.

One farmer named Boaz had seen Ruth gathering food for Naomi, and he was impressed by her compassion. She came to live among people she didn't know. She didn't have much money. She took care of Naomi.

Boaz saw Ruth and told her, "You have worked hard. Please stay with my workers. Be the first to pick what is left behind. You are also welcome to eat with us. You can come and drink water anytime you are thirsty."

"Why are you being so kind to me?" Ruth asked. "I did not grow up here. I am a stranger."

"You are not a stranger, Ruth," Boaz said. "You have been very kind to your mother-in-law since your husband died. You left everything to come here. May God bless you for your compassion. May God reward you."

"It is nice to hear kind words," Ruth said. "Thank you."

God did reward Ruth for her compassion. It wasn't long before Boaz asked Ruth to be his wife. They were soon married. Ruth had children. Ruth's family grew, and Ruth became the great-grandmother of King David.

The compassion Ruth shared with Naomi brought her to a new home. Everything was new and things were very hard, but God remembered Ruth.

God had given her food, a home, and a family. Her compassion brought her home, and it was just where she needed to be.

God wants us to be compassionate even when things are difficult. God wants us to help others even when we need help. God wants us to give even when we might need to receive.

Naomi's family left Bethlehem because there were no crops. God sent Naomi back to Bethlehem with Ruth. A new crop was growing when they came home. Compassion is like good soil. It always causes good things to grow. Maybe that's why we always need God's compassion. His love helps us grow. God's example helps us show compassion to others.

LEARNING FROM A HERO

Ruth was compassionate to Naomi. No one asked her to show compassion, but what she offered was an important gift.

1. How did Ruth show compassion to Naomi?
2. How did Boaz show compassion to Ruth?
3. How has God shown compassion to you?

Compassion means showing love and kindness to others, even when they don't deserve it.

HANNAH

Story Address:
1 Samuel 1–2

Heroic Quality:
Initiative

Be Heroic:
You, O LORD, do not abandon
those who search for you.
PSALM 9:10

Bold First Steps

Hannah was sad. She had been married for many years but had never had a child. She had a plan and believed it was the only possible way to have a son of her own to hold and love.

Once a year Hannah's family traveled from their home in the country to Shiloh to worship God. Hannah was ready to go to the tabernacle. She had been planning a special prayer.

Hannah took the initiative to walk through the tabernacle to pray to an honorable God. She may have had tears in her eyes as she began: "O Lord of all, I am overflowing with sorrow. Please hear my request for a son. If You would answer my prayer, my son will be Yours for his entire life. If You will give me the gift of a son, I will give You my son as a gift of thanks."

Hannah had thought to pray more, but the priest Eli misunderstood her tears. He thought she was making fun of God.

The sad woman was quick to say, "I was only pouring out my heart to God. Please don't think of me as wicked. My prayer comes from a heart filled with pain and sadness."

The priest seemed to understand and said, "May God give you what you desire most."

For the first time, Hannah felt as if God might answer her prayer. Sure enough, within a year she held a son named Samuel. She kept him close until he was big enough to follow directions.

Hannah kept her promise. One day she dressed Samuel in his best clothes, made sure his hair was perfect, and then took him back to Shiloh.

Nervously Hannah found Eli, the priest, and said, "I once came here praying to God to give me a son. God gave me what I asked for. I promised God that if He gave me a son I would give him back for the rest of his life. Today I keep my promise. My son, Samuel, is here to help you in the tabernacle."

Hannah worshipped God with her son, Samuel, one more time before Hannah turned to go home, leaving Samuel with Eli.

God honored Hannah's gift and gave her more children.

Her son Samuel would grow to be an important part of God's plan and was respected by all.

When Hannah left the tabernacle, she had a new prayer: "I will rejoice. God has given me strength. The holy God of Israel has rescued me. There is no one like You, God. I once had no children, but God has given me seven. He has lifted me up. He has accepted my honor. Protect me, God. Protect Samuel. Be as faithful today as You have always been. Amen."

There was no magic in Hannah's prayer for a child. She had initiative—a heroic quality that means Hannah took the first steps toward answered prayer. She was bold enough to ask God for something she really wanted. She was humble enough to give God her son. She felt strongly enough to risk being misunderstood.

Initiative doesn't have all the answers but is bold enough to ask brave questions. Initiative doesn't demand but hopes. Initiative begins when everyone else backs away. Initiative understands the answer might be no but is willing to ask just to be sure.

Hannah is a hero, not because God gave her a son, but because God was the only One she trusted to answer her biggest request. Hannah took the first steps of one with initiative, and God answered her prayer.

LEARNING FROM A HERO

Initiative is doing what you know should be done, but it also means being brave enough to try something new.

1. Why is it hard to ask God for something important?
2. How do you respond when God says no?
3. How can Hannah's story help you take more steps toward God?

When you pray, be bold, brave, hopeful, and patient. God's answers will always be best.

SAMUEL

Story Address:
1 Samuel 3, 7, 16

Heroic Quality:
Available

Be Heroic:
"Here I am. Send me."
Isaiah 6:8

Doing God's Work

Samuel was about your age when he started working in God's temple. He would do what the priest Eli asked him to do. Samuel lived with the priest.

One night when everyone had gone to bed, Samuel heard a voice call his name.

"What can I do for you?" Samuel asked. When no one answered, Samuel ran to Eli to see what he needed.

"Go back to bed, Samuel," Eli said. "I didn't call you."

Samuel went back to the tabernacle where he slept, and again he heard a voice say, "Samuel."

He was sure Eli had called him, so he ran back to the priest's room. "You called for me?"

Eli was surprised to see the boy again. "I did not call, Samuel. It's getting late. Please go back to bed."

Once more a voice said his name and Samuel ran to Eli. This time Eli knew that God Himself was talking to young Samuel. "I want you to do something for me," Eli said. "When you hear the voice speak again, I want you to say, 'I am listening. I am your servant. I am available.'"

That's just what Samuel did.

God said, "I have a message for Eli, but he will not like it. I have warned him that his family's bad choices would lead to punishment, but they refuse to make right choices. Tell the priest Eli that his sins have caught up with him."

Samuel didn't want to tell Eli the bad news, but this was the start of his new job. Like other prophets, Samuel had to say what God told him to say even if he did not like it.

Eli's reply was not what Samuel expected: "God always has a plan. He is wise and will do what He knows is best."

God spoke to Samuel when He wouldn't speak to anyone else. The messages God gave Samuel were always true.

Once Samuel had to say something he didn't like, but the people needed to hear it. "You are not following God. You serve gods that aren't real. You worship statues. You follow gods who have never helped anyone. Turn back to God and follow Him. Obey Him. Make yourself available to do what He asks. If you do this, then God will rescue you from your enemies."

God wanted the people to be available to obey Him.

Samuel always had to rely on God for wisdom. When he was asked to pick Israel's first king, he would have chosen the wrong man if God hadn't told him that Saul was the right man.

Samuel might not have looked for the second king on a hillside where a boy was watching sheep, but that's where David was found. God told Samuel, "When all you look at is how tall he is or how he looks, you have not seen his heart. I will always look at people in a different way than you do. Ask Me to help you see people the way I do."

Samuel proved he was available to do what God wanted him to do. God used him in a big way. God can use you, too.

Being a hero who is available means that you take time to learn what God says. When you know what He says, you can do what He wants. When you do what God wants, He can trust you with more. Most people will say they are too busy to help. God wants you to make time to obey.

LEARNING FROM A HERO

Samuel learned very early that God can use people who are available to be used.

1. Why do you think it would have been hard for Samuel to tell Eli what God said?
2. Why do you think God picked Samuel to choose two kings?
3. How can you be available to serve God?

When you are available to learn, God is available to teach. Be available.

JONATHAN

Story Address:
1 Samuel 18–20,
2 Samuel 1

Heroic Quality:
Trustworthy

Be Heroic:
A friend is always loyal.
PROVERBS 17:17

A Friend from the Beginning

Jonathan might have watched from his father's tent when the shepherd boy David fought a giant. When David defeated Goliath, the king wanted to talk to David. That's when David met Jonathan. He was the king's son. They became friends. They even made a promise to be best friends.

David served the king by playing music and fighting in battles. When the people cheered for David, the king was not happy.

When the king found out the prophet Samuel said David would be the next king, he was angry. King Saul wanted Jonathan to be king. Saul decided he had to do whatever it took to make sure David did not become king.

David hid from the king. He met Jonathan in secret and told him the king was trying to hurt him. Jonathan couldn't believe his father could be that cruel.

David said, "We are friends, and your father knows it. He is trying to kill me."

"My father tells me everything he plans," Jonathan said. "Why would he hide something like this from me?"

"I can't come back or I might die," David replied sadly.

Jonathan sighed. "How can I help you?"

"There is a national holiday tomorrow. I have always eaten with the king on this special day, but for the next three days I will hide in the fields. If your father is angry because I am not there, then you will know he wants to hurt me," David said. "I trust you. Please don't tell your father where I am."

Jonathan promised.

Saul was very angry that David wasn't at the special meal. He was angry with Jonathan for being friends with David. The king even told his son that he planned to kill David. Jonathan was sad and disappointed. Jonathan had to find David.

Jonathan searched for the future king out in the field. The look on Jonathan's face told David that the king really was trying to kill him. The friends cried together because David would be going away.

"Find peace as you travel," said Jonathan. "I will be loyal to you. God will help me keep my promise. We are friends, David. We are best friends."

Both men were sad. Jonathan returned to his father. David went away. He would never see Jonathan again.

Jonathan was sad every time he heard that his father decided to chase David again. Jonathan knew David would be the next king. Jonathan wanted his father to understand that this was what God wanted.

As the years went by, King Saul became angrier and meaner. David had to hide in faraway lands. Jonathan missed his friend.

When Jonathan died in battle, David wrote something to help others remember his best friend: "My friend is a hero, but his fight is over. He can fight no more, for he has fallen. My tears won't stop. I loved you, my friend."

Jonathan could be trusted. The friendship he had with David was still strong even when they could no longer see each other. Jonathan understood something his father, King Saul, never could. God is the One who decides. Jonathan never tried to become king. He trusted that God knew what He was doing when He chose David.

David trusted Jonathan. The king's son was sad that his father treated David so badly. When Jonathan learned what his father planned, he helped save his friend's life.

God wants each of us to be trustworthy. The story of Jonathan helps us see that being trustworthy makes us heroes.

LEARNING FROM A HERO

Jonathan proved he could be trusted. That's what made him David's best friend.

1. Why couldn't David trust Saul?
2. How did Jonathan's actions prove he could be trusted?
3. Why is trustworthiness something we want in our closest friends?

Being loyal and trustworthy is something that parents want, children need, and God loves.

ABIGAIL

Story Address:
1 Samuel 25:1–38

Heroic Quality:
Courageous

Be Heroic:
Be brave and courageous.
PSALM 27:14

The Courage to Say "I'm Sorry"

David was going to be king. God had said so, the prophet Samuel had said so, and King Saul didn't like it. He was jealous of David.

The future king had many friends who traveled with him to places where Saul would never think to look. Wherever David went, he tried to help anyone in need.

One day David remembered it was time for a national holiday. He was happy and wanted to celebrate with his friends, but they had very little food. That's when David saw some men taking care of sheep.

One of David's friends went to talk to the shepherds. "Hello. I'm with David. We've been staying nearby."

"Yes, we know you," said a kind shepherd.

"You also know it is a national holiday," said the man.

"Yes. We are anxious to get home," replied the shepherd.

"Since we've been kind to you, could you show kindness to us? We have nothing to celebrate this holiday. Any food would be welcome," said David's friend.

"These sheep don't belong to me, but I will ask my employer, Nabal," said the shepherd.

After the shepherd had been gone for a while, an angry Nabal came walking back with him. "Why should I give you food?" Nabal said in anger. "I will feed my workers, but not you. King Saul is looking for you. Your men are nothing more than outlaws. You shouldn't even be here. Find your own food," shouted Nabal.

Nabal had been rude to David. The shepherds knew David to be kind and helpful. David's friends knew how badly he had been treated by King Saul. They weren't surprised when David told them to prepare for war against Nabal.

Four hundred men were on their way to fight against Nabal. The shepherds were frightened and didn't know what to do. One of them hurried to talk to Nabal's wife, Abigail.

"These are kind men. They protect us and the sheep. They have been offended and are ready to fight. What can we do?" asked a shepherd.

Abigail may have been frightened for a moment, but she quickly found great courage. She smiled and said, "It is a national holiday. We have two hundred loaves of bread, five sheep prepared for a meal, a large basket of roasted grain, clusters of raisins, and some fig cakes. We will give this to David and his men. Take them to him. I will follow. I need to apologize to the future king."

"You could be killed," said the shepherd.

"We must trust in God," Abigail said. "Hurry."

A courageous Abigail soon stood before her future king. "I didn't know you sent men to ask for help. I'm sorry," she began. "Please forgive me for any wrong. God will reward you as you fight His battles—and not fight wars of revenge. God cares for you, and He can keep your life safe. Please accept my gift and find reason for joy—and not anger—on this day of celebration."

David understood forgiveness. He heard Abigail, and he forgave. The war was called off.

Abigail risked the anger of the future king, but it is a courageous act to apologize. She had come with food for a celebration. It's hard to celebrate anger. On a national holiday, a future king learned the value of kindness and forgiveness. Abigail's courage stood between a war and mercy. If her plan failed, her family would have had the worst possible day. Because of her courage, many lives were saved, and that really was something to celebrate.

LEARNING FROM A HERO

Abigail had the courage to stand before David and apologize for something she didn't do. Her courage saved her family.

1. Why did David get angry with Nabal?
2. Why did courage make Abigail a hero?
3. How can you show courage when you know you need to do the right thing?

When you are afraid, remember how Abigail's courage saved her family and prevented David from making a mistake.

DAVID

Story Address:
1 Samuel 17; 2 Samuel 9

Heroic Quality:
Kindness

Be Heroic:
If you have a gift for showing kindness to others, do it gladly.
Romans 12:8

A King Plans a Kindness

David was the youngest son in a large family. His brothers were soldiers for King Saul. David's job was watching his father's sheep.

God had already picked David to be king, but he was picked when he was a boy. He had to grow up first.

One day David's father asked him to visit his brothers to see if they were okay. David was very brave, but he was the youngest and he watched the sheep.

His brothers were not happy to see him. "Why don't you go back to the sheep?" they chided.

David knew sheep needed someone to take care of them. He had stopped a bear and a lion that wanted to hurt his father's sheep.

Suddenly he heard a loud voice saying, "Who will fight me?" The soldiers were very afraid.

David thought soldiers were supposed to be strong. David thought soldiers were supposed to be brave. David thought soldiers were supposed to protect.

David knew he had to do something about the man named Goliath. The giant was making fun of God's soldiers.

King Saul wanted to meet David. He asked the shepherd boy to put on some armor if he was going to fight the giant. The armor didn't fit. David never wore a helmet when caring for sheep, and he thought it might get in the way of fighting someone who was making fun of God's people.

David stopped by a stream and picked up five stones. He remembered the animals that tried to steal the sheep. He had used the stones and a sling before, and David served God.

Goliath made fun of David. All he could see was a boy in front of him. God saw someone who was strong, brave, and willing to protect.

God helped David defeat Goliath. That day everyone thought of David as more than a shepherd. This shepherd was everything the soldiers had failed to be.

Many years passed and David was now a man. He and the king's son, Jonathan, had become the best of friends. They promised to always be kind to each other.

King Saul was not kind to David. He was not happy when people liked David more than they liked him. He was not happy that his son was David's best friend.

One day David planned to leave because the king was so mean. His friend Jonathan told him to remember their promise to always be kind to each other. They were both sad to leave each other.

Even more years passed. The sad news came that King Saul had died. It was time for the shepherd to become king.

King David asked if King Saul had any family left. David remembered the promise he made to his friend Jonathan. A man with a very long name was brought to King David. His name was Mephibosheth. He was Jonathan's son.

This man was disabled. He had trouble walking because both of his feet were damaged. He had been this way for a long time.

David had been a shepherd who cared for sheep. He would show kindness to this man.

Each day King David ate with Jonathan's son. David made sure that Mephibosheth had everything he needed. People even said David treated the disabled grandson of King Saul like a son.

God helped David learn how to be a good king and friend. David learned many great lessons by doing something none of his brothers wanted to do. David learned to be strong, brave, kind, and willing to protect others by watching sheep. He became a hero.

LEARNING FROM A HERO

King David was kind to someone he didn't know. It is easy to be nice to people we like. It can be hard to show kindness to someone who has been mean.

1. How did King David show kindness to Mephibosheth?
2. Why did kindness make David a hero?
3. How can you show kindness to others?

When you feel like being unkind, remember how King David treated Mephibosheth.

NATHAN

Story Address:
2 Samuel 12:1–24

Heroic Quality:
Truthful

Be Heroic:
Lead me by your truth and teach me,
for you are the God who saves me.
PSALM 25:5

Special Delivery

King David was a good king. He had followed God and faced many bad days. God had used King David to do many of the things God planned.

But one day King David took something that didn't belong to him. He had no right to take it, and he lied about it.

God was not happy. He had a message for David, and it was coming special delivery.

The prophet Nathan arrived at the palace and asked to speak with the king.

"Nathan, please come in," David said. "What can I do for you?"

"Oh, King David," said Nathan, "what I have to tell you may seem a small matter, but you can be certain it is important."

"If it's important enough for you to come to see me, then I want to hear it," said King David.

"There was a poor man and a rich man," Nathan began. "They were as different as could be. The rich man had everything he could want. He owned more cows and sheep than he could count."

"I've known men like that," said King David.

"The poor man was different," said Nathan sadly. "He didn't own any cattle, and the only lamb he had was like a member of his family. He had raised the lamb since it was born and treated it like a child."

Nathan could tell the king understood how important the lamb was to the poor man.

"One day," said Nathan, "the rich man had a visitor. He wanted to be a good host, so he told his servants to make a special meal for his guest."

"That's very generous," said King David.

"True," said Nathan. "However, instead of taking a cow or sheep from his flocks, the rich man went to the poor man's farm and took his only lamb."

The king's face turned red. He was very angry. "The rich man has done the wrong thing. He has shown no kindness. He deserves to be punished. Who is this bad-mannered criminal?"

Nathan was quiet for a moment. He looked at the king and said, "You are the bad-mannered criminal."

David looked confused and guilty at the same time.

Nathan continued, "God made you the king. He gave you everything. He was prepared to give you more. But you thought it wasn't enough."

David knew that Nathan was talking about what he had stolen.

"God has told us that stealing is wrong," Nathan continued. "Yet you disobeyed. Like the rich man, you have taken what belonged to someone else and you have lied about it.

"People will know that the king has sinned, and they won't let you forget," Nathan said before he left.

King David knew he was wrong, and he asked forgiveness for his sin.

God forgave David and called him a man after His heart. Everyone will sin. Everyone will need to be forgiven. Everyone will have a reason to be sad for making wrong choices.

God needed Nathan to be the hero of truth. David needed to understand how his sin hurt other people. Because Nathan was a prophet, he spoke God's words.

For the rest of his life, David would remember the story of a mean man who stole from his poor neighbor. Every time he thought about that story, he remembered that he was that mean man. Every time he remembered, he was reminded that God forgives.

God used truth to help King David turn his back on the choice to sin and return to the God who made him king.

LEARNING FROM A HERO

People who tell the truth are heroes. God uses truth and love to help people return to God's choices.

1. Why would it be hard to tell a king he was doing the wrong thing?
2. Why is telling the truth important?
3. When it is hard to tell the truth, who can help?

Truth and love should always be used together.

SOLOMON

Story Address:
1 Kings 3

Heroic Quality:
Wise

Be Heroic:
*Get wisdom; develop
good judgment.*
PROVERBS 4:5

It's Wise to Ask

King David is the most remembered king in Israel. His son Solomon is remembered almost as much. David was a warrior. Solomon welcomed peace. David defeated enemies. Solomon built cities. David had many enemies. Solomon had many friends.

When David was very old, he chose Solomon to be the new king of Israel. Solomon knew he was different from his father. He wanted to be a good king, but he needed help.

One night Solomon had a dream. God came to him and said, "You are the new king. I will give you a gift. What would you like?"

Solomon said, "You loved my father, David. He served You faithfully. You showed Your love to my father by allowing me to become king."

The new king thought for a moment and continued, "The truth is I feel like a child. I don't know how to be a king, yet I serve a people You have chosen to bless. There are so many people in this kingdom I can't count them all. So, if You're giving me a gift, then I choose a heart that understands how to lead them. I want to know how to tell the difference between what is right and what is wrong. I can never lead these people by myself."

God thought wisdom was the perfect gift. "You could have asked to live a long time. You could have asked to be rich. You could have asked to win over any enemy," God began. "What you want is the wisdom to know how to lead My people with understanding and through just decisions. Since this is your request, I will give it. You will have the ability to understand things no one ever has before. Be prepared. I will also give you things you haven't asked for. You will be rich. You will be famous. No one will compare to you during your entire life."

These were gifts Solomon did not expect.

Then God warned Solomon, "If you want to live a long life, you will need to follow Me with your whole heart and obey My commands. Your father, David, did that. You should, too."

After this Solomon woke up. It had been a dream, but everything that happened in the dream came true. Solomon was wise. He was rich. He was famous. He lived a long life. He led his people by understanding what needed to be done next.

People would come from all over the world to see

if Solomon really was as wise as they had heard. The queen of Sheba even said, "Solomon is twice as wise as I had been told."

God used Solomon to gather wise sayings called proverbs. God used him to write poetry. God used Solomon to build His temple.

Israel lived in peace during the leadership of Solomon. This was part of the gift God had given to the king for choosing wisdom above all other gifts.

God wants to give us wisdom. He even told us, "You will need wisdom. I am generous and will give you what you need, but you must ask. I will never be disappointed when you ask for that gift."

God wants to teach us what we need to know. He is not mean. If you ask, He is willing to teach. He once said, "When you honor Me, you have taken the first step toward being wise. When you know more about Me, you will understand what you should do."

Solomon needed help to be wise. So do we. Let's ask God for wisdom.

LEARNING FROM A HERO

Solomon is the hero of wisdom. His choice of gifts proves he wanted to follow God.

1. If God offered you the same gifts Solomon could have chosen, what gift would you want?
2. Why is it important to be wise?
3. Who can help you be wise?

Solomon wanted to live a life that pleased the God who was so much wiser than he would ever be.

ELIJAH

Story Address:
1 Kings 18

Heroic Quality:
Prophet

Be Heroic:
*I will tell everyone about
your righteousness.*
PSALM 71:15

He Spoke the Truth

Being a prophet isn't always fun, but it is an important job created by God.

Elijah was a prophet. That meant he delivered messages to people from God. Most of the time those messages were not what people wanted to hear. They were also messages that Elijah didn't want to share. Many people didn't like prophets, but God's prophets spoke the truth.

The land of Israel was ruled by an evil king named Ahab. He didn't like Elijah and he didn't like listening to what he had to say.

One day Ahab saw Elijah and said, "You are a troublemaker."

Elijah said, "The only trouble I know of is the trouble you have caused. You worship something other than God. This has hurt our country. This hurts you. Bring those men who are faithful to Baal and Asherah, the gods you worship, and meet me at Mount Carmel. The true God has a message for you."

Nearly a thousand men came to Mount Carmel. There had been no rain for more than three years. No water ran through the rivers. There were no fish in the lakes. The rain had stopped when Elijah prayed, asking God to make it stop. King Ahab did not like Elijah.

No one wanted to hear the message from God, but it had been so long since anyone had seen Elijah they couldn't help themselves. They came to see the prophet.

Elijah asked, "How much longer before you make a choice? Either you follow God or you follow Baal! Which will it be?"

The men were quiet; they didn't know what to say.

This is when Elijah challenged the men. He would build an altar, and those faithful to Baal would also build one. When the altars were built, Elijah told the men to pray to Baal to see if he could start the fire underneath the altar.

The men prayed to Baal for hours, but there was no fire, not even smoke.

When Elijah had waited long enough, he told the people to come close. He asked them to pour water over his altar, not once, not twice, but three times.

The ground was soaked with water when Elijah prayed to God. Then fire came pouring from the sky and burned up the altar, the rocks, and then the ground around the altar.

Elijah proved who was the true God. Those who followed Baal were defeated.

Ahab looked at Elijah, who said, "Go get something to eat and drink because rain is coming."

Elijah had already shown the wonder of God. Now he said it would rain after more than three years of blue sky. The prophet prayed, and soon the sky changed to black. Rain began to fall. Water began to fill lakes and flow through streams.

The people had to be reminded of the one true God. Elijah told them the truth even when they didn't want to hear it. He was a prophet. He delivered his message. That's what prophets do.

God wants prophets today. The message he wants you to share is the truth found in the Bible. He wants you to take that truth and help others understand why it's an important message.

A prophet knows and shares truth. A prophet can say, "Jesus loves you." A prophet tells others, "Jesus has a better way for you to live." It may not be easy for prophets to share what they know, but prophets love God and know their message is truth God can use to change someone's heart.

LEARNING FROM A HERO

Even when he thought no one wanted to hear it, Elijah shared God's message.

1. Why do you think it would be hard to be a prophet?
2. Why would it be hard for a prophet to find a close friend?
3. Why is truth so important to a prophet?

The truth can be hard to believe, but prophets share the truth because they care about people.

ELISHA

Story Address:
2 Kings 5

Heroic Quality:
Integrity

Be Heroic:
Joyful are people of integrity.
PSALM 119:1

72

"I Serve God"

Elisha was a man of integrity. What does that mean? Well, if he were a house, he would have been built well. If he were a bridge, he would stand strong. It means that when Elisha said something, he meant it. If he told you something was true, you could believe him. What he said was the same as what he did. He was honest. He was trusted.

One day a man came to the king to be healed of a skin disease known as leprosy. Naaman was a warrior from the land of Aram. The king was frightened because Naaman expected to be healed and he had no idea how to make that happen.

He read a letter from the king of Aram that said, "Please welcome my servant Naaman. I was told you can heal him. He has gifts to show how thankful I am."

The king thought there could be a war if the man was not healed. Then he received a letter from Elisha, asking the king to send Naaman to him. God could heal the warrior. The king quickly sent Naaman away from the palace.

Naaman came to the home of Elisha but was met by a servant who said, "The prophet says to go and wash in the Jordan River seven times. If you do this, your leprosy will go away."

"Shouldn't the prophet come and see me himself?" asked Naaman. "He must have some trick or words he can use to heal me. Besides, the Jordan River is dirty. Why would I go into that river?" Naaman was angry. He had expected more from a prophet.

"It is a simple thing," said one of Naaman's friends. "The prophet asked you to do something that could heal you. If he had asked you to do something important, I think you would have done it."

Naaman decided he could lose nothing by washing in the river. One, two, three, four, five, and six times he went under the water. When he came up, the leprosy was still there. It didn't look like this was going to work, but Naaman went under one more time—and when he came up, the warrior from Aram was healed.

With pack animals covered in gifts, Naaman went back to Elisha's house. "I now believe," said the warrior, "there is no true God except in Israel. I am healed. Please accept my gifts."

Elisha was happy the man was healed, but Elisha also remembered he was not the one who healed Naaman. He just told him how to be healed.

"God healed you, Naaman. I cannot take your gifts. I serve God. He takes care of my needs."

Naaman really wanted Elisha to take the gifts, but he soon

understood that Elisha meant what he said. Elisha would not accept gifts for something he did not do.

Naaman liked Elisha's integrity. He returned to his animals and began the journey back to Aram healed of his skin disease and impressed by a prophet of integrity.

Sometimes we want to take credit for something only God can do. Elisha understood that the only One who could ever truly heal was God. Elisha served God, but Elisha wasn't God. He was honest and didn't look for a way to cheat. This was something Naaman wasn't used to. Naaman was used to people expecting payment for their good deeds. Elisha just gave the message God had given him.

People of integrity are honest about who deserves praise. For Elisha the only One who ever needed honor was God.

LEARNING FROM A HERO

Elisha wanted others to know that God is important. He wanted to show God thanks.

1. Why was it hard for Naaman to do what Elisha asked?
2. How hard would it have been to turn down Naaman's gifts?
3. How often do you thank God for all He does? Is it enough?

God loves people of integrity. Showing God honor is the most honest thing you can do.

JOSIAH

Story Address:
2 Kings 23; 2 Chronicles 34

Heroic Quality:
Cooperative

Be Heroic:
*We should help others
do what is right.*
ROMANS 15:2

The Choice to Follow

It's not easy being king when you're only eight years old, but that's what happened to Josiah. He was a good king with a heart that wanted to cooperate with God's plan. That's what made him a hero.

The people once worshipped only God, but when Josiah became king, he noticed that they were worshipping so many gods he wasn't sure he could name them all. The God who had saved them so many times was being forgotten. This made Josiah very sad.

Josiah didn't make the rule; God did. Long before Josiah was born, God said His people should never worship or serve any other god but Him. Josiah just had to cooperate with a rule God had already told the people to follow.

Whenever the young king found places where people worshipped someone or something other than the one true God, he destroyed that place. God had given Moses the rule Josiah now followed. God said, "I am God. I took you away from slavery in Egypt. You should never accept any god besides Me."

That was the rule, but few had followed the rule in a very long time.

Some people didn't agree with King Josiah, but he continued to tear down and break idols that were made to look like gods who were not real. Worshipping these gods was a waste of time, and it did not honor the one true God who really was worth obeying.

Those who knew Josiah said there had never been a king like him. He cooperated with God by turning away from sin and then following God's rules. King Josiah served God in every way he could.

The longer Josiah led his country, the more he cooperated with God. He repaired God's temple, and the people once again celebrated God's memory meal called Passover.

Then one day Hilkiah the priest found a scroll and sent it to King Josiah. When it was read to Josiah, he was so upset he tore his clothes. People used to do that when they were really upset.

The words in the scroll said that God was angry with people who didn't follow His rules. Josiah heard that God would need to punish those who thought they were smarter than Him—those who had refused to cooperate with God.

King Josiah worked hard to get rid of idols and to give people a temple where they could worship the one true God again.

Most of all, Josiah was sad he didn't know what God wanted sooner.

Josiah called all the people to Jerusalem, and there he promised to cooperate with God by obeying His rules with all his heart. He promised to pay attention to the words in the scroll the priest had found. He asked the people to do the same.

The people waited to worship other gods until after King Josiah died. It was when the people turned their backs on Him once more that God punished them.

King Josiah had shown them an example of what it looks like to cooperate with God by obeying Him. The people just didn't believe it was important.

One day the king of Babylon sent soldiers to take the city of Jerusalem. God spent seventy years teaching them that He was the one true God. This was something King Josiah knew, but the people didn't cooperate the way their king had.

God still wants heroes who will cooperate with Him today. He wants us to follow Him with all our hearts, souls, minds, and strength. Maybe you're becoming the hero God has always planned for you to be.

LEARNING FROM A HERO

God has a plan for your life. What He really wants to know is if you will cooperate.

1. Why would it have been hard for Josiah to stand up for God?
2. How can you show God you are ready to cooperate?
3. What do you like most about King Josiah?

Josiah did the right thing for the right reason. He wanted to obey God with all his heart.

HEZEKIAH

Story Address:
2 Chronicles 29–32

Heroic Quality:
Bold

Be Heroic:
Let us come boldly to the throne of our gracious God.
HEBREWS 4:16

A Powerful Decision

Hezekiah had watched as his father, King Ahaz, broke things that were used in God's temple. He watched his father close the doors to the place where his family had worshipped. He watched his father make choices that would never please God.

When Hezekiah was twenty-five years old, he became king. One of the very first things he did was to go to the temple, reopen the doors, and walk through the damaged building. Dust was thick in the temple. God's house had been abandoned too long.

After walking through the temple, Hezekiah quickly hired workers to clean and repair the building. The idols people had worshipped were destroyed. The temple tools were brought back.

The people worked hard to restore the building. In two weeks and two days, the temple was ready for worship. It had been a long time since the people had been allowed to worship here. Some had missed worshipping God. Others didn't remember God. No one had expected the temple to be repaired so quickly.

Hezekiah wanted to lead a different country than his father led. Hezekiah wanted the people to follow God with their whole hearts. The first change the people noticed was their chance to worship God in the restored temple. Their response was a wonderful celebration.

The people had to be reminded of why they worshipped and who was worthy to be worshipped. Hezekiah wrote to the people, saying, "It is time to return to the God of Abraham, Isaac, and Jacob. Our people have been destroyed by those who fought against us. May those of us who are left come back to a merciful God."

But that wasn't all. Hezekiah said, "Our relatives forgot God. They were stubborn and refused to honor God. Don't be like them. Come to His temple. Worship God here. Maybe He will stop being angry with a sinful people. Perhaps our relatives who were taken by our enemies will come home. God is kind. Return to Him. May He return to us."

People began returning to the temple to honor God. Hezekiah continued to remove everything that displeased God. All the pillars, poles, shrines, and altars used in worshipping anyone or anything other than God were destroyed.

The more the people followed God, the more generous they became. They gave gifts to God that supported the priests and their families. The extra gifts were also useful.

God was using the bold actions of a good king to help the people return to Him.

However, this wasn't the end of the boldness of King Hezekiah. One day Hezekiah was told that the king of Assyria was coming to fight him.

Assyria's king had fought other nations, and he had always won. The people were frightened. King Hezekiah stood before them and said, "Take courage and hold tight to God's strength. There is no reason to fear the king of Assyria. God's power is much greater. Yes, Assyria's king has a large army, but what is the largest army when compared to the God who can fight our battles?"

God did fight Hezekiah's battle against Assyria's king. Without a single battle, the soldiers of Assyria went home when God defeated them.

This was not the end of the problems Hezekiah and his people faced, but the boldness of doing the right thing had not only pleased God but turned the hearts of the people to the God they had forgotten.

Right choices may be hard in the beginning, but they are always choices we will be glad to remember.

LEARNING FROM A HERO

Being bold means making the best decisions using the right reason to honor an awesome God.

1. Why would it be hard for Hezekiah to restore the temple?
2. When were you bold enough to make a good choice that surprised others?
3. How can the story of Hezekiah make you bold?

When you trust God completely, it becomes much easier to make the bold decisions that please God.

NEHEMIAH

Story Address:
Nehemiah

Heroic Quality:
Purposeful

Be Heroic:
The LORD will work out his plans for my life.
PSALM 138:8

The Purposeful Builder

The people of Israel were moved to Babylon. Nehemiah worked for the king, and the king liked Nehemiah.

One day Nehemiah's brother came to visit. He had bad news from home. "The city of Jerusalem is in bad shape." Nehemiah was ready to ask more, but Hanani said, "There has been a fire. Criminals have destroyed the wall. Jerusalem is ruined."

Nehemiah's heart was broken. Jerusalem was the city of God's temple. This was a city of hope. Now it was burned, ruined, empty, and forgotten.

Day after day Nehemiah was sad. "O great God of heaven," he prayed. "You keep Your word. You love those who obey. Today I am praying and I will pray all day and night. Why? Your people have nothing to go home to because we have disobeyed You. We have not done what You commanded. We have been scattered like dust in the wind.

"You told us that if we obeyed and made the choice to live for You, You would bring us home. Some of us are following You. We want to go home, but we need a home to return to.

"O God, I will speak to the king today. Go before me and help him to be kind. Perhaps he will say yes to my request."

What was Nehemiah's request? He wanted the king to send him to Jerusalem. He wanted the king to help make sure he was safe on his journey. He wanted the king to give him the things he would need to rebuild in Jerusalem.

It would have been easy for Nehemiah to let someone else do the work, but Nehemiah saw something that needed to be done and he was willing to do it.

When Nehemiah finally saw Jerusalem, it was worse than he imagined. He tried riding his donkey through the streets, but the rubble was too thick.

It would take a long time for Nehemiah to rebuild the walls around the city by himself. Some people living nearby did not want the walls rebuilt. This was an impossible job for one man. That's why God brought other people to help.

Every day men would work to repair the gates and walls. Every day there were men who tried to stop them from rebuilding. Every day they were closer to finishing the work.

In just fifty-two days, the walls and gates were repaired. The rubble in the city was cleaned up. God had taken Nehemiah's dream and made real what seemed impossible.

The city had hope once again. Nehemiah's brother Hanani, who had told him about the broken city, was named the governor. Soon the temple would be repaired. Soon God's people would come home.

Nehemiah knew that his purpose was to do more than just work for a king. He didn't always know how he could finish what God asked him to start, but he kept praying, working, and believing.

Most people would say that Nehemiah had no idea how to rebuild. They might have been right, but when God gives you a job, He will always help you get the job done.

God gives everyone a purpose. We each have something that only we can do. What we can do is God's gift to us, and it's a gift we can give others. When we know why God made us, we can finally do our jobs well.

Nehemiah was a hero of purpose. When he knew what he was supposed to do, he could ask a king for help and the king would help.

LEARNING FROM A HERO

It's hard doing something no one else will try. When you know God's purpose, you never have to be afraid.

1. Why would it be hard to ask the king for help with something that wasn't your job?
2. How did knowing his purpose change Nehemiah?
3. How did Nehemiah's work bring hope to the people?

Purpose is knowing what you're supposed to do and doing it.

ESTHER

Story Address:
Esther 1–5

Heroic Quality:
Brave

Be Heroic:
*"Do not be afraid or discouraged.
For the Lord your God is with you."*
Joshua 1:9

The Family Hero

Esther hadn't planned on being a queen. She was just a normal girl living a regular life when the king held a contest for a new queen. She won.

Esther was happy just being normal. King Xerxes had asked his workers to find beautiful young ladies. That's how she became a contestant.

She wasn't sad being queen. Things just happened so fast. Her close relative Mordecai had been giving her advice on how to be wise, and she was happy she could talk to him. The king had never met Mordecai even though Mordecai had once saved the king's life.

One of the king's men named Haman hated Mordecai.

He wanted Mordecai to treat him as if he were the king; everybody else did. Mordecai refused to bow when Haman walked by. The more Haman thought about it, the more he wanted Mordecai to be punished.

That's when Haman had a very bad, very terrible idea. Haman told the king, "There are people in your kingdom who are very different. They do not follow your laws, and they keep away from other people. You never know what they will do. They really shouldn't be allowed to live. If you sign a law that these people should die, I will give you ten thousand sacks of money."

The king should have asked more questions before he signed the new law. Within a year every one of Mordecai's family members would die—including Queen Esther.

When Mordecai heard this news, he went to speak with Esther. She was sad and very frightened. That's when Mordecai said, "You must go to the king and ask him to stop this from happening. We will all die. Even you won't escape."

Esther wished she was a young girl who wasn't queen. Life was easier then.

"I can't go to the king unless he asks for me," Esther said. "If I were to go to the king uninvited, he could have me killed."

"If you don't go to the king, we all will die," Mordecai said sadly.

"The only way this can happen is if the king welcomes me by holding out his golden staff," Esther said.

"Then we all will pray for you," said Mordecai.

Soon Esther was at the king's door. She was frightened but knew she must be brave if she wanted to help her people.

She walked into the room. The king looked at her. All was quiet for a moment. Esther wasn't sure she was even breathing. Then? The king smiled and held out his golden staff.

It took a lot of courage to go to the king, but Esther

needed even more courage. That's why she waited to ask the king for help. She invited him and the evil Haman to two banquets. It was at that second feast that Esther told the king what Haman had done and that if the law wasn't changed she would die.

The king did not want to see his queen hurt in any way. He was very unhappy with Haman for what he had done. After all, Mordecai had discovered that two men were trying to hurt the king, and he had been honored for being heroic by exposing them. Now Haman wanted this hero to die because Mordecai had hurt his feelings.

Because the law couldn't be changed, the king signed a new law allowing Esther's people to defend themselves if anyone tried to hurt them. Her family was spared.

Being brave is doing the hard thing just when it needs to be done. This is why Esther will always be a hero.

LEARNING FROM A HERO

Esther didn't choose to be queen, but God knew she was brave.

1. Why didn't Esther want to go to the king?
2. When you have a hard choice to make, how can you be brave?
3. What story can you tell that helps you remember what it's like to be brave?

Sometimes God asks us to be brave. We can do what He asks because He's always with us.

MORDECAI

Story Address:
Esther

Heroic Quality:
Prepared

Be Heroic:
*You prepare a feast for me in
the presence of my enemies.*
Psalm 23:5

The Right Choices

King Xerxes was a very famous king. He made the rules for people to follow, and a lot of people followed him.

One of the men who lived in his kingdom was Mordecai. He worked for the king and was a relative of the queen. King Xerxes did not know that.

Mordecai was working one day when he heard two men talking. Bigthana and Teresh also worked for the king, but they were angry with him. In fact, they were so mad they planned to kill the king. Mordecai knew it was important to let King Xerxes know his life might be in danger. He spoke to the queen, and then Esther told the king.

When the king found out that Bigthana and Teresh really did plan to hurt him, they were in big trouble. The whole story was written down in the king's book. Then Mordecai went back to work.

One man who didn't like Mordecai was Haman, who thought he himself should be treated like a king. When Haman saw that Mordecai would not treat him in a special way, he went to the king and told him that there was a bad family who lived in the kingdom. This was a lie, but the king believed Haman and made a rule that would hurt those people. Mordecai and Queen Esther both were part of that family.

Mordecai told Queen Esther what she must do to help.

Haman was happy he had tricked the king, but Mordecai prayed.

One night the king couldn't sleep. He asked one of his helpers to read some of the stories written in the king's book. The helper read a few stories and then read how Mordecai saved the king from Bigthana and Teresh.

"Did we ever tell him thank you?" asked the king.

"I don't think so, sir," said the helper.

"Ask Haman to come in," said the king.

Haman came into the room. He was still angry with Mordecai.

"Haman, what should I do to show honor to someone I think has done a very good job?" asked the king.

Haman could not think of anyone who had done a better job than himself. "Well, if you really want to honor someone special, I think you should let that person wear one of your royal robes while riding on one of your own horses. Someone the people know should lead that man through the streets. To make it even better, the person leading the horse should let people know that this is what the king does for someone who does a good job."

The king smiled and said, "That is an excellent idea. I want you to do everything you just said for Mordecai. He saved my life, you know."

This was not what Haman expected. He wanted Mordecai to be punished, but now he was going to be honored.

Haman was angry because he had to show honor to Mordecai in front of everyone.

The king soon learned that Mordecai was a relative of the queen. He showed him even more honor.

Haman wanted to make people laugh at Mordecai, but God had other plans. Mordecai had learned from God that obedience helped prepare him for God's best.

Mordecai is the hero of preparation because he made the choice to do the right thing for the right reason. That preparation helped him serve God, save lives, and rescue the king.

Prepare for tomorrow by obeying God today.

LEARNING FROM A HERO

We show God how much we love Him by being prepared to follow Him—anywhere.

1. How can you prepare to follow God?
2. Why would it have been hard to stand up against Haman?
3. How did preparation help Mordecai become a hero?

Being prepared is what helps you do what God created you to do.

JOB

Story Address:
Job

Heroic Quality:
Patient

Be Heroic:
*Be still in the presence of the Lord,
and wait patiently for him to act.*
PSALM 37:7

Bad Day Survival

Job was a good man. Job was a rich man. Job was a man who followed God.

One day the devil came to see God.

"Where have you been?" God asked.

"I've been watching what happens on earth," said the devil.

"Then you've noticed Job. He serves Me well," God said.

"But you're the One who protects him. You've made him rich. If You were to stop helping him, then Job would stop doing the right thing," said the devil.

Job had done nothing wrong, but the devil soon destroyed most of the things Job owned.

Job couldn't understand why bad things were happening to him, but he honored God even in those bad times.

It wasn't long before Job was sick with disease. It seemed that everything that could go wrong had gone wrong.

Three of Job's friends came to visit. They found Job sitting in the dirt. They weren't used to seeing this. Job had been one of the richest men they had ever known. They thought he must have done something really bad to be punished like this. They thought God was angry with Job, but God wasn't punishing Job.

The three friends sat with Job for several days. They didn't say anything. Job was happy for friends who would comfort him in silence.

Imagine how hard it would be if everything you owned were taken away and you didn't know why. You would be sad. This was how Job felt. He thought his friends understood.

Job finally said something, but he may have wished he had kept his thoughts to himself. "I was always afraid something bad like this would happen. Now it is true. I cannot find peace and I cannot rest. Trouble has come to live with me. I wish it would leave."

Job's friend Eliphaz thought he knew what was wrong, so he told Job, "I've heard some angels are bad. If God can't trust every angel, then how can He trust you? People face hard times every day. You should admit your sin to God before you are crushed."

Job tried to tell them he had done nothing wrong, but every time he spoke, one of his friends would blame him for breaking God's rules.

Not only was Job sad, but he was a little angry. He might have even wished his friends would go home and leave him alone.

God was showing the devil there really were people who followed Him even when things weren't easy, but Job didn't know what was happening. He patiently waited for God to help him understand.

God finally did help Job understand, but He was not happy with Job's friends. God said, "You three don't seem to know Me as well as Job does. You deserve to be punished for thinking you had all the answers. You were just guessing. Ask Job to pray for you. I will accept his prayer."

After Job had been patient for so long, God blessed him and gave him a life that was good because it included family, friends, and best of all, the love of God.

Job was the hero of patience. He didn't know what God was doing, but God trusted Job. God wanted Job to trust Him. Bad things do happen to people who make good choices, but God tells us that He can make good things come from our worst moments. We just need to know God, love Him, and follow Him—even on the bad days.

LEARNING FROM A HERO

Sometimes we just don't understand what God is doing. That's because we're not God. His plans are always perfect.

1. How would you feel if you were Job?
2. What will you remember most about Job's story?
3. Who is always patient with us?

The story of Job can help us remember that no matter what happens, God never stops loving us.

ISAIAH

Story Address:
2 Kings 20; Isaiah

Heroic Quality:
Hopeful

Be Heroic:
We put our hope in the LORD.
He is our help and our shield.
PSALM 33:20

The Way of Promise

A prophet can only say what God tells him or her to say. Isaiah was one of many prophets, but his book is longer than most of the others. Like Ezekiel, he shared words that seemed harsh and sad, but Isaiah also shared words that told people what the Messiah would be like. God told him to speak about Jesus hundreds of years before Jesus was born.

Isaiah shared God's messages when Ahaz was king. Ahaz was an evil king and did not honor God. Isaiah shared God's messages when Hezekiah was king. Hezekiah was nothing like his father. He loved God and served him faithfully.

Isaiah was a prophet before Daniel was taken to Babylon, before the temple was abandoned, and before Nehemiah rebuilt Jerusalem's city walls.

King Hezekiah often spoke with Isaiah. Even though Hezekiah was a good king, he made a big mistake. A group of important people from Babylon came to see his kingdom. Hezekiah was so proud he showed them everything. This included all the gold and silver used in worshipping God.

Isaiah told the king that Babylon would come back someday and take all the temple tools back to Babylon. They would also take some of the people.

The best message Isaiah could share was one the people didn't understand, because it was something that would happen in the future.

As with most of the prophets, Isaiah's real message was, "We need to be rescued." But it would take a long time for people to understand the hope Isaiah had to share.

Isaiah said the Messiah would be born to a virgin, and Jesus was born to a virgin named Mary.

Isaiah said the Messiah would be a relative of King David. Jesus was in the family tree of David.

Isaiah said someone would prepare the way for the Messiah. John the Baptist made sure everything was ready for Jesus.

Isaiah said the Messiah would pay for sin. Jesus paid for our sin.

Isaiah said the Messiah would be rejected. Jesus was rejected.

Isaiah said the Messiah would accept the punishment for our sins. Jesus accepted our punishment to pay for our sin.

Isaiah said the Messiah would bring salvation. Jesus brought salvation.

Isaiah said God's Spirit would be with the Messiah. Jesus had the Spirit of God.

Isaiah's book was written during the time of brave men, but also men who were disobedient. He was friends with other prophets who shared God's message. Isaiah is not always thought of as a person who shared a message of hope. Maybe that's because the people didn't understand who Isaiah was talking about.

Isaiah once told the people, "God says He will make the heavens and earth new. We will forget the old ones. God will make Jerusalem a place of happy days. God's people will bring Him joy. There will come a day when no one will know what weeping and crying sound like. Babies will grow strong and people will live a long time. People will own houses and work hard. People won't steal, and God will bless them. When they pray, God will answer before their first word. This is a hope-filled day worth waiting for—and it is coming. Be patient. Someday will be here before you know it. You can believe because God said so."

Isaiah was not a gloomy preacher, but a prophet of hope.

LEARNING FROM A HERO

God chose Isaiah to help people understand that hard days always point to a God who rescues.

1. Why is it important to hope in God?
2. When do you need the most hope?
3. How is hoping different from wishing?

Hope asks you to trust in a God who has already proven that He can be trusted. God's plans always end well for those who hope in Him.

JEREMIAH

Story Address:
Jeremiah

Heroic Quality:
Dedicated

Be Heroic:
*Restore to me the joy of your salvation,
and make me willing to obey you.*
Psalm 51:12

Operation Obedience

The prophet Jeremiah was dedicated. He delivered hard messages for God. However, when God gave Jeremiah the job, Jeremiah did not think he was the right person. He said, "Lord, I am a young man, and I would not know what to say."

God replied, "There's no reason to worry, Jeremiah. I can use anyone, even if he is young. I will give you a message. Share it with people. Do not be afraid. I will go with you."

Jeremiah was not sure he could do this job. God continued, "I am touching your mouth so you can easily say my words."

When God made Jeremiah a prophet, the people of Judah had a good king named Josiah. Jeremiah said God was angry that the people were worshipping Baal instead of God.

Good King Josiah was working hard to remove all idols from his country, but Jeremiah still said God would judge His people and they would be sent to another nation to live.

Why would God judge a nation when the king was doing his best to do the right thing?

King Josiah followed God, but the people would not. They kept worshipping idols. They kept sinning. They kept pushing God away.

When King Josiah died, the people once again worshipped idols whenever they wanted. The next four kings didn't follow God like King Josiah did.

Suddenly Jeremiah's message from God made more sense, but the people were tired of hearing it. Every time Jeremiah shared God's message, people got angry. His brothers attacked him, a priest tried to punish him, and one of the kings didn't like his message and put Jeremiah in jail. Some people tried to kill him, he was tossed into a well with his feet stuck in mud, and many people said Jeremiah was lying.

Some called Jeremiah the "Weeping Prophet." It must have been hard for him to tell people what God had to say when they wouldn't listen. Each day for weeks, months, and years, Jeremiah spoke for God. It seemed his warnings did no good.

On the day Jerusalem was invaded by the king of Babylon, the people of Judah may have finally believed that Jeremiah was really sharing God's words.

Babylon's king told his soldiers to find Jeremiah and treat him with great kindness. When the commander of the Babylonian army found Jeremiah, the prophet was in chains. The commander immediately set him free.

He looked at Jeremiah and said, "Your God said disaster would happen here, didn't He?"

Jeremiah nodded his head.

The commander looked at the people who had refused to listen and said, "What happens here today is because you would not obey God. I am freeing a true prophet, and he can go wherever he likes."

The commander made sure Jeremiah had food and water. After so many years dedicated to speaking God's message, Jeremiah began a journey to a friend's home where he lived with those who were allowed to stay in Judah. Everyone else was taken to Babylon.

Someday the people would come back. In the years that followed, Jeremiah wrote the story of his life, the deeds of the kings, and the sadness he felt knowing that God's message was ignored. Even when he wrote, God gave him the words.

Today we read Jeremiah's story in the Old Testament. This prophet shared God's message every day. Jeremiah's dedication allowed truth to be shared even when everyone believed a lie. God was pleased with the prophet and understood why he was sad. God was sad, too, but one day He would bring His people home.

LEARNING FROM A HERO

Jeremiah was dedicated to sharing a message that no one liked. God gave him this job.

1. Why should we obey God even when others don't think it's important?
2. Jeremiah was young. What did he learn about following God?
3. Why is it important that God's message is true?

Being dedicated means making the choice to follow God. He's always with us, for us, and in us.

EZEKIEL

Story Address:
Ezekiel

Heroic Quality:
Preacher

Be Heroic:
Encourage your people
with good teaching.
2 TIMOTHY 4:2

Three Special Messages

Many people had been taken from Israel to Babylon. More would be taken. Daniel was one of the first to leave his country. Eight years later Ezekiel was taken, but he had a message that God wanted him to preach.

Babylon wasn't anything like Jerusalem. Some people who came from Israel now acted just like the Babylonians. Others just wanted to go home.

God said to Ezekiel, "Stand up and listen. Israel refuses to follow Me. They only do what they want to do. They are so stubborn. Even when you give them My message, they won't listen to you because they have not listened to Me. They may threaten and scowl, but you must speak for Me. When I give you a message, you must preach."

Ezekiel preached his first sermon: "God called you, but you refuse to listen. There is war and sickness. Disaster has come. Money can't save you when God is angry, and He is angry. Other people will take what you own and you will be frightened. The king cannot help you. You have sinned. Punishment is here. Your only hope is to remember God."

The people didn't like Ezekiel's sermon, but he could only preach what God told him to say.

After Ezekiel preached to the people of Israel, God asked him to preach to the people who didn't like Israel. "You cheered when Israel was led away into Babylon," he began. "Didn't you see that God's people were being destroyed? He will be the judge between your response and His plan. You will come to honor the true God."

These people didn't like Ezekiel's sermon, but he could only preach what God told him to say.

There came a day when Ezekiel's sermon gave the people hope.

"This is what God says," Ezekiel told the crowd. "You don't deserve it, but I will bring you home. I am holy and I want to make you clean. You will come from wherever you are. The land you used to know will be the land you will know once more. You have had a hard heart for too long. I can and will give you a new, tender heart. You have been punished, but now you will be rescued. You will once again obey My commands. You are My people, and I am your God."

This was the best sermon most of the people had ever heard. God was coming to the rescue and things were going to change. Ezekiel preached what God told him to say, and this was a sermon he liked sharing. God hadn't left them. He hadn't forgotten them. Israel had been punished because of sin. When all they had known was taken away, they finally remembered the God who had been forgotten.

God needed someone who would tell the people of Israel just what He wanted them to know. Not everyone would do that. Ezekiel was a preacher willing to speak God's words. The sermons weren't always encouraging, and sometimes they made people sad, but the sermons also made people remember the God they were supposed to follow.

It takes a hero to tell others the truth. For Ezekiel this meant he told the truth that the people would be punished. He preached to other countries to remind them that God was not pleased that they made fun of His people. Finally, Ezekiel could tell the people that the punishment would end. They were going home, and the people found new reason to honor the God who rescues.

LEARNING FROM A HERO

Ezekiel had a hard job. He could preach only what God told him to say.

1. Why was it hard for Ezekiel to be a preacher?
2. What would you do if God wanted you to share His truth?
3. How would your life be different if you could only speak God's words?

We should tell others about God. Like Ezekiel, we should share what God says in the Bible.

DANIEL

Story Address:
Daniel 6

Heroic Quality:
Confident

Be Heroic:
*My heart is confident
in you, O God.*
Psalm 57:7

Accused but Confident

Daniel was the wisest man in all of Babylon. More than one king had asked him for help, and Daniel was very helpful. This made other people unhappy, because they wanted the king to like them, too.

When King Darius asked for help, many people wanted the job. Three were given the best jobs, but Daniel was always wiser and more trustworthy. The king was going to make Daniel the top ruler. The only person with more power than Daniel would be the king. This made some of the people angry. The others were jealous and wanted the job Daniel was getting.

"Can anyone think of something Daniel does wrong?" asked one of the men.

After thinking for a while, another man replied, "He's always been faithful to the king, responsible to do his job, and everyone trusts him."

"That's true," said another, "but maybe we can find a way to make Daniel look bad."

"What do you mean?" said the first.

"As you know, Daniel isn't from Babylon. He came here when he was young, and he prays to God," said the man. "What if we made it a crime to pray to anyone but the king?"

The men all laughed, because they were certain they had finally found a way to make Daniel look bad.

King Darius heard the plan. He agreed that it was a good idea. Everyone would be required to pray only to him for thirty days. The king did not think this new law would hurt Daniel, his wise and trusted friend.

After everyone was aware of the new law, Daniel prayed to God, just as he had three times each day for years. He was arrested and taken to the king.

The king could not break his own law. He had to punish Daniel, but the punishment he had agreed to when he made the law was something he no longer wanted to do. The law said that anyone who broke this rule would be thrown into a den where hungry lions lived.

King Darius was heartbroken when he told Daniel what his punishment would be. "May the God you serve be faithful. Perhaps He can rescue you from lions."

Daniel was led away, and the men who

didn't like Daniel seemed to win.

That night King Darius could not sleep and he would not eat. He could only think about his trusted friend Daniel.

Who could survive a night with lions? the king thought, but early in the morning King Darius went to the lions' den and called out, "Daniel! Was your God faithful? Did He save you from the lions?"

"Long live the king!" Daniel called out from below. "My God sent an angel to keep the lions' mouths closed. I am not hurt. I do not even have a scratch."

"Your God is powerful," said the king.

"He rescued me because I am innocent in His sight, and I trusted Him, O King," said Daniel.

"You are innocent," said the king. "Hurry," he called to the guards, "help bring him up out of the den."

Daniel was confident that following God was the most important thing he could do. He believed God could be trusted and that no matter what happened, doing the right thing for the right reason was the right choice.

No matter how hard it may be to do what God asks you to do, remember that the same God who shut the mouths of lions is the God who can help you through tough days and hard choices.

LEARNING FROM A HERO

Daniel wasn't always confident in what other people did, but he was always confident in the faithfulness of God.

1. Why is it hard to be confident when you have to make a hard choice?
2. Who did Daniel say was responsible for his rescue?
3. How can following God make you confident?

You can always be confident when the God you trust has always been faithful. Follow Him always.

SHADRACH,
MESHACH, ABEDNEGO

Story Address:
Daniel 1, 3

Heroic Quality:
Exemplary

Be Heroic:
I have chosen to be faithful.
Psalm 119:30

They Stood Strong

Daniel had been taken to Babylon. He missed his home, but he had friends. Three of his closest friends were Shadrach, Meshach, and Abednego. These friends were smart, healthy, and strong.

When they first came to Babylon, the king was kind. He offered them the same food he ate. The king wanted these young men to like him, follow him, and serve him.

All four men asked if they could eat the same foods they had eaten before they had been taken to Babylon. The people who served the king were afraid to let them because the king had given an order.

Finally, it was agreed that the four men could eat the foods they were used to for ten days, but if they looked unhealthy in any way, they had to stop.

After ten days Daniel, Shadrach, Meshach, and Abednego all looked healthier than the other young men. They could keep eating the foods they had eaten in Israel.

The Babylonian king saw that these four men were very smart. They learned things very quickly. All four men became officials for the king.

One day the king started to build something just outside of town. Slowly a ninety-foot-tall gold statue was finished. The people were impressed by how tall the statue was. They thought it was a statue worth honoring.

The king hired someone to tell the people, "No matter where you have come from, what language you speak, or who you are related to, the king has a command for you to follow. A talented band will play a special song. When you hear the song, you will bow down and worship the statue the king has built. If you don't worship the statue, you will be thrown into a furnace."

Shadrach, Meshach, and Abednego knew they couldn't worship the statue. God had been clear when He said that His people could only worship Him. They would follow God.

Soon the talented band played the special song. People all over the city began to bow to the statue. The king was pleased. However, some people saw that Shadrach, Meshach, and Abednego did not bow down. They told the king.

The king was angry with the three men but decided to give them another chance to worship the statue. The men said, "We cannot serve any other god or statue. We will only serve the one true God. We cannot defend ourselves, but God can rescue us if you throw us into the hot furnace. A second chance will not help. We cannot bow to this idol."

An angry look came over the face of the king. He said in a loud voice, "Make the furnace seven times hotter than usual. Bring me the strongest soldiers. These three will be thrown into the furnace today!"

The people saw the flames of the furnace when Shadrach, Meshach, and Abednego were thrown in.

Wait. Hadn't they thrown in three men? Why were there now four walking around inside the furnace? Why hadn't they died? Why did the fourth man look like he should be worshipped more than the tall statue outside of town?

Suddenly the king knew he was wrong. He called the men out of the fire. They came and stood before the king. They had not been burned, and they didn't even smell like smoke! The king was amazed. The king gave them new jobs. The king worshipped their God. The tall statue was forgotten.

God wants us to follow Him. Our good example can help others be bold enough to follow.

LEARNING FROM A HERO

Sometimes following God can be hard, but Shadrach, Meshach, and Abednego knew God could be trusted.

1. Why is it easier to do what everyone else does?
2. Why is it important to be a good example?
3. How will you make a choice to be a good example today?

God wants us to make choices that help others see Him in us.

GABRIEL

Story Address:
Luke 1

Heroic Quality:
Messenger

Be Heroic:
Sing to the LORD. . .proclaim the
good news that he saves.
PSALM 96:2

This Is Good News

It was time for God to show the world His rescue plan for all people. Jesus was coming, and He would pay the price for sin. This was big news, so God sent Gabriel, a messenger angel, to make sure everything was ready.

Gabriel had seen the best and worst choices people could make. He knew God was never pleased when people disobeyed His commands. The messages that Gabriel had to deliver would start God's plan to rescue people from their sin. This was good news, yet God knew so much more about the plan than Gabriel.

Gabriel was to deliver two messages. The first was to a priest named Zechariah who was in the sanctuary burning incense to God. The priest was the only one who was supposed to be in the sanctuary, but the angel stood near the altar. When Zechariah noticed him, he was afraid.

Gabriel said, "There is no reason to be frightened, Zechariah. You have prayed for a son, and God has heard your prayer. Your wife, Elizabeth, will have a son. His name will be John. He will have an important job. He will make sure people understand the Messiah is coming. The prophets spoke of your son when they said there was one who would prepare the way of the Lord. John will share wisdom and good news, and people will listen to him."

Zechariah was very surprised. Was it really possible that he would have a son? After all, he was old. Yet the angel had said his son would help people understand that the Savior was coming.

Zechariah's wife was expecting her son, John the Baptist, when Gabriel delivered his second and most important message. Mary was soon to become the wife of Joseph. She lived in Nazareth and was looking forward to her wedding.

Gabriel was sent to visit with her. "Hello, Mary," he said, "God has a special job for you. He is with you now."

Like Zechariah, Mary was frightened.

"Do not be afraid," said Gabriel. "You will have a son. He will be the forever King."

Mary wasn't sure how that could happen since she wasn't married yet. She was very confused.

Gabriel answered the question Mary hadn't even asked. "This baby will be God's Son, and He will be holy. This is God's promise, and God never fails."

The angel's promise was enough for Mary. "I serve God," Mary said. "May what you say come true." Mary had a lot to think about.

Gabriel's messages had been delivered. Two boys would soon be born. One would make sure people were ready for God's new message.

One would change the world.

Zechariah remembered the visit from the angel and would say, "My son, John, will make preparations for God's rescue plan. People will soon see salvation in the God who forgives. God has a plan to give light to those whose choices are dark and who live through hard times. God is bringing peace. God is showing mercy."

As John and Jesus grew to be men, Gabriel must have realized just how important his message was. His news helped others look for Good News. John's news helped others find Good News. The message Jesus brought changed lives, softened hearts, and allowed all people to become friends of God.

This all started when God sent Gabriel with the message, "There is no reason to be frightened. God has heard your prayer."

LEARNING FROM A HERO

Gabriel was an angel who delivered messages. His greatest message announced the birth of Jesus.

1. Why was it hard to meet an angel?
2. What if no one believed Gabriel's message?
3. Why does God want us to share His message with others?

When you know good news, it is always good to share it. God gave us enough good news to share something new every day.

MARY

Story Address:
Luke 1–2; John 19

Heroic Quality:
Willing

Be Heroic:
Mary responded, "I am the Lord's servant."
LUKE 1:38

Ready and Willing

Augustus was the emperor of Rome. He wanted to know how many people lived in his kingdom. He made a rule that all people had to go back to the towns where their families came from. Everyone had to be counted and then had to pay a tax.

That didn't sound like fun. That didn't sound convenient. This rule was hard for Mary and her husband, Joseph. Mary was pregnant and had to travel with Joseph to Bethlehem just days before her baby was to be born. Then, when they got to Bethlehem, they discovered there was no place for them to stay.

An angel had told Mary she would give birth to God's Son, Jesus. She was willing. She wasn't sure having a baby in a stable was her plan, but it was God's plan. So in a noisy, busy, and crowded city, Jesus was born.

Mary wrapped Jesus in cloths to keep Him comfortable. He slept in a place where cows were fed, called a manger.

Mary was willing to do everything God asked her to do, but Mary didn't always understand.

Before Jesus was born, Mary said, "My soul knows God is great. My spirit finds joy in Him. Somehow God picked me to give birth to His Son. He is mighty. He is holy. He is kind. He has always been this way. God is strong. He is never pleased with pride. He loves humble people. He wants rich people to trust Him and not their money. I want to remember His kindness. I want to remember His faithfulness. I want to remember His goodness. I will remember."

Mary didn't know the answer to every question. She knew God had all the answers. If she was willing to follow, God could help her understand the answers.

Mary watched Jesus grow. Mary watched Jesus work with His earthly father, Joseph. Mary saw that Jesus was just as kind and faithful as God had always been.

Jesus was born for a reason. She knew He would save people, but she didn't know how.

Mary watched Jesus teach His disciples. She saw the miracles He performed. She was there when Jesus hung on the cross.

This was not her plan. This was not what she wanted. This made her very sad.

As Mary watched, Jesus looked at her with great kindness. Then Jesus looked at one of His disciples. "John," Jesus said, "I want you to be like a son to Mary. She will be like a mother to you. Take care of her."

Mary must have cried when she realized Jesus was dying. John stood beside Mary at the cross, and then he took her home to live with him. John took care of her.

Mary had been willing to do everything God had asked, but watching Jesus die was so hard for her. She was the mother of God's Son.

Good news. Jesus did not stay dead. He had come to save people, just as Mary had been told. Nothing like this had ever happened in history.

Sometimes being willing to do something isn't easy. You might be asked to do things that are hard and unpleasant. You might be asked to believe things you don't understand. You might be asked to give up things you really want.

Jesus was willing to save us. Mary was willing to be the mother of God's Son. God is willing to rescue. Are you willing to admit you need to be rescued?

LEARNING FROM A HERO

Mary is a hero who showed us over and over that God uses people who are willing to obey.

1. Why is it sometimes hard to obey your parents?
2. How are things different when you're willing to obey?
3. Why is being willing important?

God wants to use you to do something special. Are you willing?

JOSEPH

Story Address:
Matthew 1; Luke 2

Heroic Quality:
Committed

Be Heroic:
I havo chosen to be faithful.
PSALM 119:30

Faithful Obedience

Joseph was ready to take Mary to be his wife. Then he found out Mary was chosen by God to be the mother of God's Son. Mary was going to have a baby boy.

Joseph didn't know what to do. He thought about breaking off their engagement, but an angel came to Joseph in a dream and told him to take Mary to be his wife. Joseph followed God's directions.

God was the father of Jesus. Joseph was chosen to help take care of God's Son as He grew up. Joseph worked hard to take care of his family.

When Jesus was eight days old, Joseph and Mary took Him to the temple to be dedicated. While they were there, two wise elderly people, Anna and Simeon, recognized Jesus as the Messiah. Joseph couldn't help but wonder at God's best gifts.

Later wise men arrived. Joseph welcomed them as they honored Jesus.

King Herod heard of the wise men's visit. The wise men had said they were looking for an infant king in Israel. The king didn't want anyone to be more important than he was. He created a new law that said all baby boys under the age of two should be killed.

An angel appeared to Joseph and told him where he should go. Joseph used the wise men's gift of gold to take his family to Egypt where they would be safe.

After the king died, the family returned from Egypt. They lived in Nazareth. Jesus was a healthy, strong, and wise boy. Mary and Joseph were proud of Him.

Jesus was twelve years old when the family traveled to Jerusalem for the memory meal known as Passover. Jerusalem was where God's house was located. Most people called it the temple.

It was a great celebration. When it was over, Joseph and Mary and many others began the long trip home. They didn't notice Jesus wasn't with them. Many of the children would play together on the journey, so Joseph and Mary thought He might be with them. Joseph couldn't find Jesus. Mary couldn't find Jesus. No one had seen Him since they left Jerusalem.

Joseph and Mary went back to Jerusalem. They looked in all the places they had been during the celebration. They looked in places where they hadn't been. Then they heard Jesus' voice. He spoke as if He were the wisest person who ever lived.

Jesus was in the temple teaching religious leaders things they didn't know about God.

Joseph and Mary didn't want to interrupt, but they needed to get back on the road to Nazareth.

Mary said, "We have been looking for You everywhere. We were so worried. Why did You stay behind when You knew we were going home?"

Jesus looked kindly at His mother and said, "You really didn't need to search. I thought you knew I would be in My Father's house."

Maybe Joseph remembered that Jesus was God's Son. Maybe Mary remembered, too.

Jesus obeyed Joseph and Mary and went home with them.

Joseph taught Jesus the skills he knew, and Jesus learned well. Jesus had a heavenly Father. Jesus also had an earthly father committed to God's plan. Joseph looked after Jesus and helped Him in any way he could. He took Mary to be his wife. It must have been hard, but Joseph obeyed God and remained faithful to what God had asked him to do.

Jesus wants us to be committed. Commitment starts with a willingness to obey.

LEARNING FROM A HERO

Joseph followed God's directions when it seemed easier to ignore them.

1. Why is it hard to do something you don't want to do?
2. Why does Jesus want us to be committed?
3. How can you be more willing to do what God wants?

Sometimes God might ask us to follow a plan that doesn't make us famous or popular. God would rather see us obey than become proud.

JOHN
THE BAPTIST

Story Address:
Matthew 3; John 3:27–36

Heroic Quality:
Humble

Be Heroic:
*Humble yourselves before the Lord,
and he will lift you up in honor.*
JAMES 4:10

Less Important

The angel Gabriel had promised the priest Zechariah that his wife, Elizabeth, would have a son. God's promise was true. Their son, John, grew up, but he was very different from most young men.

God had given John a very important job. He was to make things ready for Jesus.

Most people wouldn't think of the desert as a place to tell people about Jesus, but that's just what John did, and people came to hear what he had to say.

"You must stop breaking God's rules. Turn around, and don't be friends with sin," he said. "God's kingdom is almost here."

Some people came to hear John speak. Others came because of the way he looked, for he wore clothes made from the hair of camels and held together with a leather belt. For lunch he ate locusts and honey he found in the desert.

There was something very different about John.

Some of the men who worked in the temple came to hear John speak, and he told them things they didn't want to hear. Other people came to hear him because he talked about something that would happen that would surprise everyone.

"Soon One will come who is much more important than I will ever be," John began. "He will come with God's Spirit. I am not even worthy to be His servant."

Then Jesus walked out of the crowd and John recognized that Jesus was the One he had been telling people about. Jesus wanted John to baptize Him.

"If anyone should be baptized today, it should be me," John said.

"You have prepared the way, and God has asked Me to be baptized," Jesus said.

He was amazed. The Messiah had asked John to baptize Him. Jesus went under the water, and when He came up, something wonderful happened.

God's Spirit came on Jesus. Some said the Spirit looked like a dove. A voice came from heaven and said, "My Son pleases Me, and I love Him."

People had followed John. People had loved John. People were not sure what to do now that they had met Jesus.

Those people who had followed John the Baptist wondered why he didn't go out to the wilderness to preach like he used to. John told them, "My job was to tell people about Jesus. I am happy to see what He is doing. As He becomes greater, I must become less important. He is greater than anyone who has ever lived. Jesus is from heaven, and God sent Him. Jesus is the Master of everything, and His message is better than anything I have ever preached. I had a job, but it's done. Follow Jesus."

A man named Andrew had followed John the Baptist, but John encouraged him to follow Jesus. Andrew became one of Jesus' disciples. So did his brother, Simon Peter.

John the Baptist was a man people wanted to hear. More and more people came to hear him speak. Yet when Jesus came to meet him, John the Baptist was humble enough to step back because the message Jesus had to share was much more important.

John could have continued to preach, but he knew his job had changed. He had prepared the way for Jesus, and Jesus was rescuing people, changing lives, and showing God's love. John pointed people to Jesus.

John could watch and give thanks to God. Jesus had come to rescue people from their choice to sin. John made sure everything was ready. John had been faithful. God was pleased.

LEARNING FROM A HERO

John the Baptist was a humble hero. When Jesus showed up, John stepped back.

1. Why is it hard to let someone else do something you enjoy?
2. How do you know John the Baptist was humble?
3. How did John the Baptist obey God?

John the Baptist wanted what God wanted. He helped when God asked and stopped when God's Son arrived.

JESUS

Story Address:
Luke

Heroic Quality:
Loving

Be Heroic:
All glory to [Jesus] who loves us
and has freed us from our sins.
REVELATION 1:5

A Life of Love

Jesus had always been God, but He had never been a baby. He had never been just like us.

But He became just like us. It wasn't because He was curious. It was because He loved us.

Sometimes parents tell their children something that is true, but the children won't believe it until they see it. From Jesus' first cry until He died on the cross, Jesus showed everyone what real love looks like. He brought truth. Many believed.

From the beginning God knew that all people would need the rescue plan of salvation. Why? God gave us rules, but people couldn't keep them. When they broke a rule, God called it sin. God said the only thing a person could earn from sinning is death. The worst part about breaking God's rules is that you can't be close to God.

Jesus loved us so much that He came to do something no one expected. The rescue plan Jesus came to fulfill was the most amazing plan ever, and it would only work if Jesus never ever broke God's rules.

God's greatest enemy, the devil, tried to get Jesus to break the rules, but Jesus never did.

At the time Jesus was born, people sacrificed animals at the temple to be forgiven for breaking God's rules. The only sacrifice God would accept to pay for all sin was someone who was perfect. Someone who had never broken His rules. The only perfect human was Jesus.

Most people liked Jesus. He made sick people well. He made crooked legs straight. He brought people who had died back to life.

More than once Jesus fed people. They liked that, too. He took a few fish and some bread and somehow made it enough for thousands of people to eat.

Some people wanted to make Jesus their king, but Jesus came to do something far more important.

A man named Judas had followed Jesus, but he was not a good friend. He went to men who did not like Jesus and told them where to find Him. He told them he would take them. He told them he would no longer be Jesus' friend.

Men who worked in the temple said Jesus wasn't following the rules, but Jesus was the only One who ever did follow all of God's rules. Those same men who said horrible things about Jesus also said that He should die for breaking the rules.

This was wrong. The men were wrong. Jesus was perfect. Jesus did not do anything to earn a death sentence. Yet Jesus went to the cross. He was perfect. He did not break the rules. Yet He died.

For three days the friends of Jesus were very sad. The men who worked in the temple thought they had done a good thing. His mother cried.

But when Jesus died, God accepted His sacrifice as the only way people could be forgiven. Don't be sad. More good news was coming.

Jesus did not stay dead. Jesus is alive! He is proof that God's rescue plan was perfect. Men, women, and children could now be close to God all the time. They didn't have to stay away. God offered life with Him in heaven.

Bad news became good news. Death became life. Sadness became rejoicing. Sin met forgiveness. Jesus had shown love to everyone.

That was a good day. No, that was the best day!

LEARNING FROM A HERO

Jesus came to rescue people by dying to pay for the rules we break. This was something only love could do.

1. Why is it so hard to keep all God's rules?
2. What surprises you most about the story of Jesus?
3. How do we know Jesus loves us?

Jesus died to rescue us, lives to keep us close, and is planning a wonderful future for us.

JOHN
THE DISCIPLE

Story Address:
Mark 5; Luke 22

Heroic Quality:
Sincere

Be Heroic:
You must show sincere love to each other. . .with all your heart.
1 Peter 1:22

A True Friend

John's job was catching fish. That was before Jesus dropped by his boat. John followed Jesus.

Like the other disciples, John had seen many miracles. He learned a lot from listening to Jesus.

Sometimes Jesus had a special place to go, and John was often invited to go with Him. Peter and his brother, James, were also invited to come.

The first time Jesus invited the three to come with Him was on a busy day when a little girl was sick at home.

Jesus had already healed a man. Then as He was on His way to see the girl, He healed a woman. While Jesus was busy, the little girl died.

Jairus was the little girl's father. He waited while Jesus spoke to the woman who was healed. He was sad when a friend came through the crowd and told him, "You don't need to bother Jesus anymore. Your daughter is dead."

Before Jairus could even think, Jesus told him, "There is no reason for fear. This is a time to believe."

The crowd had seen miracles, and they wanted to see more. Jesus stopped the crowd but asked John, James, and Peter to come with Him to see the little girl.

Everyone was sad at the house of Jairus. John followed Jesus into the house.

Then Jesus said something that made the people laugh: "Why is everyone so sad? The little girl is only asleep."

Jesus knew the people would not understand. He asked them to go back to their homes. That's when John, James, and Peter followed Jesus to the room where the little girl lay on her bed. Her father and mother were sad as they looked at their daughter.

Jesus took the child's hand and said, "Little girl, it is time to get up."

There were gasps of welcome surprise when the girl who had been dead opened her eyes, sat up, and began walking around the room.

Jesus smiled and looked at Jairus. "You should get her some food. She's probably hungry."

This was what it was like when John followed Jesus. He saw over and over how much Jesus loved people.

Once when Jesus came into Jerusalem for the memory meal known as Passover, the people shouted, "Hosanna!" They threw palm branches on the ground so His donkey didn't have to step on the ground. They honored Jesus, and John was so pleased that he followed this great man.

Later Jesus asked John and Peter to make sure they had everything they needed to remember how God saved His people. That's what people did in the memory meal.

John followed all the directions Jesus had given. The meal was served. The disciples could see something was different about this meal. Jesus talked about His body being broken for people. He talked about sacrifice. This meal would be remembered for new reasons. Jesus was talking about what He would go through on the cross.

John didn't know it, but this would be the last meal he would share with Jesus before Jesus died.

John is the hero of sincerity. His love for Jesus was serious. He was truthful in sharing what Jesus had done for him.

John would be used by God to write several books in the Bible, including the Gospel of John and the book of Revelation. John was genuine, devoted, and true in following Jesus.

Jesus wants us to be that kind of hero.

LEARNING FROM A HERO

John was a disciple who was devoted to following Jesus.

1. Why is following Jesus important?
2. How can you show that you want to follow Jesus?
3. What can you do to remember all the important things Jesus has done for you?

John is known as the disciple Jesus loved. John had a close friendship with Jesus. So can you.

JAMES
SON OF ZEBEDEE

Story Address:
Matthew 4; Mark 14; Acts 12

Heroic Quality:
Loyal

Be Heroic:
*Never let loyalty
and kindness leave you!*
PROVERBS 3:3

Loyal to the End

James looked at his brother, John. He had also noticed the man walking along the beach. Their father, Zebedee, was repairing nets. They planned to fish again in the morning because that was their job. Fishing. Every day. There were good days with lots of fish and bad days when there were none, but the nets always needed repair. Hauling in nets as the sea rocked the boat back and forth was the only job they knew, but they got a promotion when the man on the beach stopped and said ten life-changing words.

"Follow Me, and I will make you fishers of men," Jesus said.

He didn't tell them why they needed to follow. He didn't tell them what to expect if they did follow. He didn't tell them whether they would ever come back to the boat, the nets, and the fishing. He didn't even explain how they were supposed to fish for men.

Jesus just gave them an invitation and then waited for their response.

Both James and John left the boat and followed the preacher. Others would join them.

Twelve men were invited, and each gave up everything to follow Jesus, to learn His commands, and to grow in His love.

James saw Jesus perform miracles. He saw Jesus heal sick people and bring the dead back to life. James listened to Jesus' stories, shared meals with Him, and heard Jesus preach sermons that changed his way of thinking many times.

Jesus was different than other people who talked about God. Other people could only talk about God as if He could just be found in a history book. Jesus talked about God as Someone He knew. The disciples were amazed at the difference.

The disciples were all with Jesus at His last supper. He washed their feet. He spoke about things they couldn't quite understand yet. Then Jesus asked James to come with Him because He needed to pray. John and Peter were also invited.

The three disciples were so tired they couldn't stay awake while Jesus prayed. They were still sleepy when soldiers came to arrest Jesus. The disciple named Judas had betrayed Him.

So many good memories were swallowed up by the sad betrayal. The three disciples ran away frightened.

It wasn't long before Jesus was killed on a cross, placed in a tomb, and then rose from the dead.

Like all the disciples, James needed to be forgiven. The love Jesus gave allowed James to tell people everywhere he went about Jesus. He really had become a fisher of men. The message he shared could change lives. The hope he had inspired people. The love God gave was poured out like water on people who needed it most.

Some people didn't like the news that Jesus could rescue people from sin. In time, King Herod arrested James because he shared Jesus' good news. He was the first disciple to be killed for following Jesus.

If he could do it over again, James would have left his father's boat once more to follow Jesus, because it was Jesus who changed his life. It was Jesus who gave him a future beyond earth. It was Jesus who forgave him when he ran. James's life changed—because of Jesus.

We are asked to follow Jesus today. We may think other plans are more important, but Jesus invites us to follow Him, and when we do, we will learn that we have accepted the best future ever.

LEARNING FROM A HERO

James is remembered as loyal to Jesus. He may have failed from time to time, but James loved Jesus.

1. Why is it important that James and John followed Jesus?
2. Why would it be hard to watch Jesus being betrayed?
3. Jesus wants you to follow Him. How will you respond?

God asks us to be loyal to Him, and then He gives everything we need to stay loyal.

LUKE

Story Address:
Luke, Acts

Heroic Quality:
Friendly

Be Heroic:
*A real friend sticks
closer than a brother.*
Proverbs 18:24

Historical Friendship

Luke wasn't at the stable when Jesus was born. Luke wasn't a disciple. And Luke was not like most people in Israel.

Luke was a Gentile. This meant that he was someone who wasn't from the family of Abraham. Most people in Israel didn't like Gentiles.

Jesus said He came to rescue all people. That included Gentiles. No one expected that. People always thought the Messiah would save only the family of Abraham.

Luke was a doctor. He helped sick people get well. Once he learned about Jesus, known as the Great Physician, he started a new job. God chose Luke to write history books.

Sometimes people think history books are boring, but the first book God helped Luke write is the best book for learning what the first Christmas was like.

If you look in your Bible, you will find his books, Luke and Acts. Both help us learn about history. The first book is a history book about Jesus' life. Luke talked with people who had been at each event he wrote about. He made sure he did the research so his history books were trustworthy. Some events and stories about Jesus can only be found in Luke.

The second book Luke wrote is a history of the earliest churches. That book is called Acts. This time Luke lived through most of what he wrote about. He was a missionary friend to Paul. Some people say he helped Paul when he was sick.

Luke wanted people to understand that Jesus came to offer His rescue plan of salvation to everyone. Luke helped people see that Paul and his friends left Israel and shared God's best news with people who had never heard of God.

Jesus said He came to make things new. He came to give us a new way to think. He came to forgive us.

God gave Luke the skills to write the words we would need to read so we could understand how Jesus changed history.

Luke was a hero God used to show that He really does love everyone.

Sometimes we can think that God only loves some people. Luke was from a family that some people thought God couldn't love. Luke proved that Jesus didn't want to keep people out. Jesus loved Luke as much as any of His disciples. Luke showed everyone that God could and would use anyone. God accepted Luke.

When you know God accepts you, it's easier to share what you're learning. That's what Luke did, but he used words so we could learn.

How exciting would it be to talk to people who actually saw the miracles of Jesus? This is what Luke was allowed to do. He heard the parables or stories that Jesus told from the people who first heard them. He wrote about miracles. He wrote about mission trips. He wrote about how God was changing the lives of people wherever he went.

We can read about the people who met Jesus. Luke got to talk to them.

We can only imagine what it was like for the disciples. Luke could just ask.

We can wonder if Jesus smiled a lot. Luke was told more than he wrote down.

God gave Luke a job, and it was a great job.

Luke must have had many friends, because he spoke to many people about Jesus. He wrote because God asked him to write.

LEARNING FROM A HERO

Good friends know how to talk and listen. Luke must have been good at both.

1. How much would you enjoy talking to people who met Jesus?
2. Why do good friends listen to what you have to say?
3. Why is it important to be a good friend?

God used Luke to share the history of Jesus. God wanted us to know He can be a friend to anyone.

MARY
AND MARTHA

Story Address:
Luke 10:38–42

Heroic Quality:
Worshipful

Be Heroic:
Come, let us worship and bow down.
Let us kneel before the LORD our maker.
PSALM 95:6

Just a Little More Time

Mary and Martha were sisters. Both wanted to show honor to Jesus. He was coming to visit them soon.

Martha spent her time in the kitchen. She wanted the meal to be special when Jesus arrived. Mary wasn't interested in cooking. She just wanted to see Jesus. She kept looking out the window to see if He was close. Martha was not happy with Mary.

When Jesus finally arrived at their house, Mary was the first to greet Him. Martha was busy cooking while Jesus taught His disciples. Mary sat nearby, listening and honoring Jesus with her attention.

To worship Jesus means we set aside time to honor Him. We want to show Him gratitude. We want to show that we love Him.

So who worshipped Jesus? If you said Mary, you're right. If you said Martha, you're also right.

Both sisters worshipped Jesus. Mary worshipped by spending time with Him and showing Him honor and gratitude. Martha worshipped Jesus by serving Him. She wanted to show Him that she was grateful and that she loved Him.

But Martha thought she was the only one worshipping Jesus. She was doing all the work while her sister just listened to Jesus. Martha wanted to talk with Jesus about her sister. "Lord," she began with a frown, "maybe You've seen Mary. She has been sitting with Your disciples, listening to what You say. It seems unfair that I should do all the work while she does nothing. Please tell her to help me."

Jesus looked at Martha kindly and said, "You are so worried about details. You are upset that I might not be able to eat on time. Martha, your sister has learned that there is only one thing that is really worth so much attention. She honors Me with her time. She has been doing something, and I accept her honor."

Martha probably didn't want to hear what Jesus said, but it helps us understand that Jesus wants us to spend more time getting to know Him than serving Him.

Honor and service are both ways we can worship God, but He wants us to know Him first so we can serve Him better. Sometimes we think if we just do more for God, then He will love us more. He tells us that He already loves us and wants to spend time with us.

He loves to see us serve Him by helping others. He loves it even more when we show how much we love Him by spending time with Him. We can do that by reading more about Him, praying to Him, or asking questions about Him.

Sometimes when we work hard, the only thing we think of is the work we're doing. When we spend time talking to Jesus and reading His words, we are thinking about what He wants us to do. This is why Jesus said that the way Mary worshipped Him was the best way.

Mary sat, listened, and learned. Martha cooked, worried, and got upset.

Mary showed honor. Martha showed anger.

Mary showed love. Martha showed frustration.

Worship is something God looks for in a hero. It takes a hero to know that he or she doesn't know everything, can't prepare for the unknown, and will never need to claim a trophy to be loved by God.

Heroes know they can help, but they also know that without God nothing gets done.

This was something Mary knew and Martha learned.

LEARNING FROM A HERO

God wants heroes who will honor Him and learn from Him.

1. Is it easier for you to do something or learn something?
2. What does it mean to worship God?
3. Why do you think it's easier to do things for God than to spend time with Him?

God wants heroes to worship Him with their time as well as their talent.

GOOD SAMARITAN

Story Address:
Luke 10:30–37

Heroic Quality:
Accepting

Be Heroic:
Accept each other just as
Christ has accepted you.
Romans 15:7

Surprised by Acceptance

Jesus was the best storyteller ever because His stories always helped people live better. One story most people remember is about the Good Samaritan. This story was strange to those who first heard Jesus' words, because He spoke of a Samaritan as being good, but the people listening didn't like Samaritans. This is important because some thought Jesus only cared about a few people. Jesus wanted them to know He cared for everybody—including Samaritans.

There once was a man who traveled from Jerusalem to Jericho. There were no cars, so he had to walk. It wasn't long before bandits rushed him and took his money. He had been hurt when they robbed him and was lying on the side of the road, too injured to move.

He needed help, and he hoped someone would show up soon.

Within a short time a priest walked along. Surely a priest would help the injured man.

Maybe the priest was busy. Maybe he was in a hurry. Maybe he was frightened. When the priest saw the man, he hurried to the other side of the road and walked on without saying a word.

The injured man was from Jerusalem. Did he know the priest? Maybe the priest didn't recognize him with his injuries.

The poor man's strength was running out when another man came walking along the road. This was a man who worked in the temple; surely he would stop.

He did stop, for a minute. He looked at the injured man. Maybe he was trying to think what he could do. Maybe he wondered if the man could pay for his own care if he did help him. Maybe he just thought it was unusual.

But just like the priest, the temple assistant walked to the other side of the road and hurried on.

The injured man had no money, no one seemed to care, and he was running out of hope.

Wait! Did he hear the sound of hooves on the road? Was there a horse coming? Would he be rescued?

His heart sank when he saw that it was a Samaritan. If the priest and the temple assistant walked by, then he was sure the Samaritan wouldn't help. His nation had never gotten along with people from Samaria.

Imagine his surprise when the man stopped. He looked over the man. He grabbed medicine. He unrolled bandages. The good Samaritan put the injured man on his donkey.

As quickly as the donkey could safely travel, the Samaritan took the man to an inn and paid for his care. He promised to come back and pay for anything else that was needed.

This was the story Jesus told those who followed Him. When the story was over, Jesus said, "The injured man met a priest, a temple assistant, and a Samaritan. Which of the three was a good neighbor to the man who had been attacked?"

It didn't take long for the followers of Jesus to agree, "The good Samaritan."

Jesus asked, "Why?"

One of Jesus' followers replied, "He was the only one who accepted him."

Jesus must have smiled as He said, "That is true. Please go and treat people the same way."

It's important that Jesus helped those who followed Him understand that they could accept others because He accepted everyone. Jesus showed that even those we may have thought were bad can show compassion. Sometimes they can show better manners than we do.

Jesus came for everyone, and everyone can come to Jesus.

LEARNING FROM A HERO

Kindness can come from people we least expect. Accepting others is a hero quality God created.

1. Can you name a way you can accept someone today?
2. Why was this story important for Jesus to tell?
3. How can others like us if we refuse to accept them?

When God sends help from unlikely people, it is the perfect time to thank Him for accepting and loving us.

NICODEMUS

Story Address:
John 3; 7:50–51

Heroic Quality:
Inquisitive

Be Heroic:
*Teach the righteous, and
they will learn even more.*
PROVERBS 9:9

Night School

Nicodemus was a religious leader known as a Pharisee. He had been paying attention to what Jesus was teaching. While other Pharisees did not like what Jesus said, Nicodemus wanted to learn more.

One night after dark, Nicodemus came to see Jesus. He called Jesus a rabbi. This name means "teacher," and it was a sign of honor. Nicodemus was letting Jesus know he wanted to learn from Him.

"I believe God has sent You to teach us. I have seen and heard of Your miracles. What You do proves God is with You."

Nicodemus might have expected Jesus to thank him or ask what He could do for him, but Jesus told Nicodemus what he needed to know. "Here is a truthful message. You can never truly understand God unless you are born twice."

Nicodemus was confused. People were only born once. They were babies only once. How could anyone be born twice?

Jesus knew the Pharisee was confused. He said, "You can be sure that no one is welcome in God's kingdom without being born twice. God's Spirit gives birth in a human heart to the real life God wants for His people. We are all born once. Only with God's help can you be born twice."

"I don't understand," said Nicodemus.

"I am surprised," said Jesus. "You are a respected teacher of God's laws. I thought you would understand. I will tell you something else you will not understand, but someday you might. God loved you enough to send His only Son to live among you. God wants people to escape death by believing in His Son. Forever life is coming, and God will not be angry with anyone who believes in His Son. But He will judge those who refuse to believe."

"How will we know God's Son when He comes?" Nicodemus asked.

"When He comes into this world, people who are evil will hide from His teachings. They will hide in the dark like animals who will not show themselves in the light. They will be afraid that He will show everyone how wrong they have been. But those who are willing to learn will search for God's Son so they can learn what God wants them to do."

Nicodemus left thinking a lot about what he had learned. God sent His Son. God wants people to believe in His Son. God's Son has the wisdom to teach people. Suddenly Nicodemus had a new thought, "Could Jesus be God's Son?"

One day the Pharisees were more upset with Jesus than usual. They wanted to arrest Him. Nicodemus could see the religious leaders were not thinking the right thoughts. He spoke up and said, "Can we judge a man before he is put on trial?" It was a good question, but no one listened.

In time the Pharisees did arrest Jesus. They convinced the government to crucify Him. They watched Him die.

Nicodemus would remember the words of Jesus: "Forever life is coming, and God will not be angry with anyone who believes in His Son." He had learned what it means to be born twice. He learned that Jesus was God's Son. He wanted to learn more about Jesus every day of his life.

God has given us His book, the Bible. It has all the information we need to learn about Him. He wants us to learn. The best way to learn is to read what God has already told us.

LEARNING FROM A HERO

Nicodemus learned more about Jesus by showing he was interested. God is never afraid of questions.

1. What is a serious question you would like to ask God?
2. How can you show honor to the God who is willing to teach?
3. What can you do to learn more about Jesus today?

God is ready to teach—when we're ready to learn.

SIMON
OF CYRENE

Story Address:
Mark 15

Heroic Quality:
Servant-like

Be Heroic:
*"The greatest among
you must be a servant."*
MATTHEW 23:11

"Let Me Help You"

Jerusalem was celebrating the memory meal known as Passover. Jesus had eaten the meal with His disciples. Judas had betrayed Jesus. Peter denied he knew Jesus. A crowd gathered to watch God's Son be crucified. The normal tradition of Passover was forgotten. New memories would be made that day.

Simon of Cyrene had no idea what was going on inside Jerusalem. He was coming to the city with his two young sons, Alexander and Rufus. They had laughed and told stories and talked about so many things. The journey had been long, but they enjoyed being together.

When they came through the gates of the city, Jesus was carrying His cross through the streets. Some people were quiet as He came by. Others shouted at Him and called Him names.

Simon came to where the crowd was gathered and saw Jesus stumble. He was weak. The cross was heavy.

The soldiers told Jesus to get up. Jesus tried but couldn't. The soldiers were not patient.

"You," one of the soldiers said, pointing at Simon. "Come here."

Simon didn't know Jesus. He had planned to spend time with his sons. This was supposed to be a happy visit to Jerusalem.

Simon asked his sons to stay together, and then he stepped forward as the crowd moved to the side. The soldier looked at Simon and said, "This man is too weak. You will need to carry his cross to that hill over there. To the place called Golgotha."

Jesus looked at Simon with great kindness. Simon took the cross from the shoulder of Jesus, and they began to walk toward the hill.

Simon may have wondered what Jesus had done. Maybe he had heard of Jesus and was sad to see what was happening. Perhaps Jesus said something that comforted Simon.

Step by step the cross was dragged to the hill. One by one the crowd gathered to watch.

Carrying a cross was not something Simon would have imagined doing that day. A cross was something for criminals, but Jesus was not a criminal. People were punished for being bad, but Jesus was good. Justice was supposed to win, and that day it did. Jesus came to rescue people from sin, and His sacrifice meant that God could forgive.

Simon could not understand what had happened. He could not explain it to his sons, Alexander and Rufus. However, Simon had served God's Son. Simon would be remembered for helping Jesus give people the great gift of mercy.

Simon of Cyrene met Jesus. Simon didn't feel like making fun of

Him. Simon didn't feel happy that a good man was going to die. Simon served Jesus when He was asked.

It all started as a trip to the city, but when a person meets Jesus, things always change.

God wants us to serve Him well. Sometimes we may be asked to do things that are fun. Sometimes we may be asked to do something very hard.

God has said, "Be loyal in serving Me. Use your whole heart to worship Me. I have done some wonderful things for you. Think about that. That's when you can understand how to follow Me even better."

We should serve God because we love God. God uses people to do His work, and God's work always includes people.

Jesus came to rescue us from our sin. Jesus came to love people and show them how to be forgiven. Jesus uses people to share that good news with other people.

LEARNING FROM A HERO

Serving Jesus is the greatest job we can ever have. When we choose to do something for Him, it is always a good choice.

1. How did Simon of Cyrene serve Jesus?
2. Why is it important to serve Jesus?
3. How can you serve Jesus today?

Simon served Jesus. We can serve Him, too.

JOSEPH
OF ARIMATHEA

Story Address:
John 19

Heroic Quality:
Generous

Be Heroic:
*Good comes to those who
lend. . .generously.*
Psalm 112:5

144

An Unusual Gift

Joseph was from Arimathea. He was a member of the high council and was honored and respected. He was waiting for God's kingdom and believed Jesus was the Messiah—the One who could save.

Joseph did not usually tell others what he believed, because the religious leaders did not like Jesus. In fact, some of those leaders arrested Jesus. Some of those leaders wanted Pilate, the governor, to give Jesus a death sentence. Some of those leaders paid Judas, one of Jesus' disciples, to betray Him.

Soon Jesus stood silent before the religious leaders who accused Him of things that weren't true. Jesus stood before the governor, who told the people Jesus was innocent. Jesus was quiet when the crowd started yelling, "Crucify Him!"

Joseph of Arimathea hoped that people would stop and think about what they were doing. Jesus was innocent, but the people still cried, "Crucify Him!"

Pilate offered to let either a murderer or Jesus go free, but the crowd screamed, "Crucify Him!"

Joseph watched in shame as Jesus was unfairly punished. Joseph felt sadness as he watched Jesus hanging from the cross. The choice to kill Jesus was not right. Jesus had done nothing wrong.

Joseph may have even heard Jesus say, "Father, please forgive these people. They don't know what they are doing."

Some people laughed and made fun of Jesus. Some people cried because they knew a wrong decision was made that day. Most people were confused.

When Jesus said, "It is finished," His body grew still. The sky grew dark. Rain fell. An earthquake shook the ground.

Then it was over.

People were quiet when they returned home. They didn't know what to say. They didn't know what to do. They didn't know how to act.

While most people were sad, Joseph quietly went to visit Governor Pilate and asked, "May I have the body of Jesus?"

"Why?" asked Pilate.

"I was told Jesus has no tomb. I will give him mine," Joseph said.

Pilate thought everything over and said, "You may bury Jesus."

Joseph prepared Jesus for burial in a tomb he had purchased for himself. When he was finished, the stone that stood before the tomb was rolled back in front of the opening and Jesus' body was left alone inside.

Soldiers came to guard Jesus' tomb because the leaders thought someone might steal His body.

On the third day, Jesus no longer needed Joseph's gift of a tomb.

Jesus had risen from the dead. He had paid the full price God demanded for the forgiveness of sin. Jesus had defeated death, and people never had to be separated from God again.

The strips of cloth that Joseph wrapped around Jesus were loose and empty. The large stone at the entrance of the tomb had been rolled away. The soldiers had all gone home. Jesus was alive. God's great rescue plan had worked just as He promised.

Joseph was only one of a few religious leaders who understood Jesus was more than a great teacher. He wasn't a troublemaker. He wasn't mean. Jesus had answers to questions people hadn't thought of yet. He had come to save people from sin. Too many people thought the Messiah would come to make sure no one would fight them anymore. They didn't understand why Jesus came.

Joseph was generous. His gift meant the body of Jesus was safe.

The good news of salvation was about to be shared. Joseph of Arimathea always had one of the best stories to share. We still share it today.

Don't look for Jesus in Joseph's tomb. He's not there. Jesus is alive!

LEARNING FROM A HERO

When everyone else turned away, Joseph of Arimathea gave Jesus a funeral.

1. Why is it hard to give something that is really important to you?
2. How did Joseph show he was generous?
3. If being generous shows that we love people, then how can we be more generous?

Joseph gave up his tomb. Jesus gave up His life. They both were generous, and God was pleased.

PETER

Story Address:
Matthew 14, 16, 18, 26;
John 21

Heroic Quality:
Grateful

Be Heroic:
Give thanks to the Lord,
for he is good!
Psalm 106:1

Forgiveness Appreciation

Peter was a fisherman. He knew how to catch fish. He knew how to fix broken nets. He knew how to work on boats.

Peter was also a disciple of Jesus.

Sometimes Peter made promises he couldn't keep. Sometimes he did things before he thought about whether he should. Sometimes he said things that got him into trouble.

One night Jesus went to pray alone. The disciples got into a boat and headed toward the other side of the lake. The disciples were caught in a storm in the middle of the night. The waves were making it hard to get to the shore. Then they noticed Jesus walking on the water. The disciples were afraid.

Peter asked Jesus if he could walk on water, too. Jesus told Peter to get out of the boat and walk to Him. It wasn't long before Peter started to sink. When he stopped trusting Jesus, he needed to be rescued.

Once Jesus asked His disciples who people thought He was. He asked Peter who he thought He was. Peter said, "You are the Son of God." Jesus told Peter he was right. Then Jesus said, "Peter, I will use you to build My church."

Sometimes Peter said the right thing. Sometimes Peter did the wrong thing.

Peter wanted Jesus to say he was generous. That's why Peter said, "I would be willing to forgive someone seven times for offending me. That's enough, isn't it, Jesus?"

Jesus said, "That's a start. You should continue to forgive them even after you stop counting how many times you've forgiven them."

Peter thought he was being generous by being willing to forgive someone a few times. Jesus showed Peter he would need to be forgiven—often.

When Jesus was betrayed, Peter ran away. When Jesus was on trial, Peter lied three times. When people asked if he followed Jesus, he said no. He said he didn't know Jesus. He asked people to stop asking him so many questions.

The third time Peter lied about knowing Jesus, he raised his head and saw Jesus looking at him.

Peter felt horrible. He did not deserve to have Jesus love him. He did not deserve forgiveness. He had made a mess of things.

Peter needed to be forgiven even after Jesus stopped counting how many times He had forgiven him.

Jesus died on the cross, and Peter was certain he had failed the Son of God.

Then one day after Jesus had risen from the dead, Peter saw Him on the shore. The disciple had gone fishing, but nothing else mattered when he saw Jesus. Peter jumped into the water and went to see Jesus. He didn't know what to say. He wasn't even sure Jesus would talk to him.

"Peter," Jesus began, "come and eat."

Jesus made breakfast on the beach, and the disciples ate with Him.

When the meal was over, Jesus spoke once more to Peter. "Do you love Me more than the other disciples do?"

"I do love You," Peter said.

"Then I want you to take care of those who follow Me," Jesus said.

Jesus asked Peter the same question two more times. Peter was sad that Jesus had to ask if he loved Him. Maybe that's when Peter understood that Jesus had forgiven him. Jesus wanted Peter to take care of those who followed Him.

Peter had been forgiven for so much. Jesus taught him to love others. Peter was grateful that Jesus gave him another chance.

Jesus had been generous with Peter, and Peter would be grateful for the rest of his life.

LEARNING FROM A HERO

Peter loved others because Jesus forgave him. No wonder he was grateful.

1. Why can it be hard to be grateful?
2. How can forgiveness make us grateful?
3. Why do you like to be forgiven?

Forgiveness means that nothing can come between you and the love of Jesus.

PAUL

Story Address:
Acts 9–12

Heroic Quality:
Teachable

Be Heroic:
*Faith comes from hearing. . .
the Good News about Christ.*
Romans 10:17

Saul did not like Jesus. Saul did not like people who followed Jesus. Yet Saul had not met Jesus.

One day when Saul was going to Damascus, he was blinded by a bright light. He couldn't see where he was going so he fell down, wondering what had happened.

"Why are you trying to hurt Me?" a voice asked Saul.

"Hurt You? Who are You?" Saul asked.

"My name is Jesus, and you have been hurting the people who follow Me. Listen carefully to what I have to say. Go to Damascus. Once you are in the city, you will be told what comes next."

Saul had heard everything Jesus said, but the friends who were with him did not. They helped Saul walk to Damascus.

Jesus had another message to share. This time He visited a man named Ananias who was a follower of Jesus. "Ananias," Jesus began, "take a walk down Straight Street. Find a man named Judas. He will know where you will find Saul."

Saul wanted to arrest the followers of Jesus, so Ananias did not want to meet him.

"The man named Saul is praying to Me," Jesus said. "I have told him you would be coming to help him see again."

"Jesus, this man has been chosen by the religious leaders to arrest anyone who calls on Your name," Ananias said.

"You must go. Saul is the man I have chosen to take My good news to the Gentiles. He will share My message with kings. He will share My message with the family of Abraham. His life will not be easy, because he is the least likely person to share the hope only I can give."

Ananias obeyed. He prayed for Saul and Saul was healed.

Now that Saul could see, there was much to learn and much to do.

It was hard for people to trust Saul. They remembered how he had arrested Christians. Now he wanted to share God's good news. He became a Christian, but most people thought it was a trick.

Then Saul became friends with Barnabas. They went on a missionary journey together. Far away from Jerusalem, no one knew Saul. They could listen to the Good News without thinking about what Saul had done in the past.

New people were following Jesus. Saul, who was now also called Paul, was learning how to follow, how to teach, and how to lead. He did not learn everything right away. He learned, and then he shared what he learned. He grew, and he shared how to grow. He loved, and he shared how to love.

There were times Paul was put in prison for being a Christian. This is the exact punishment he once hoped would happen to anyone who followed Jesus. Even in those bad days in prison, God used Paul to write books we find in the Bible.

Paul was not stingy with what he learned. He was willing to share what he knew. God would use Paul to write words like, "It is good to rejoice because God has done great things. Always rejoice."

Paul also wrote, "When God is on our side, we win."

Because Paul allowed Jesus to teach him, he became willing to share what he learned. God used Paul to write more than a dozen books in the Bible to help us learn, too.

Paul was teachable. When he met Jesus, Paul's future changed. Paul understood that Jesus could change the hearts, plans, and lives of anyone. That's a great lesson.

LEARNING FROM A HERO

When Paul met Jesus, he became a student. The rest of his life he learned how to follow.

1. What are some of the new things you're learning about Jesus?
2. How does it help to have Christian friends?
3. Why would it have been hard to trust Paul before he met Jesus?

Jesus wants us to be His students. He wants us to learn and share what we know.

BARNABAS

Story Address:
Acts 13–14

Heroic Quality:
Encouraging

Be Heroic:
Encourage each other and
build each other up.
1 THESSALONIANS 5:11

The Power to Encourage

God never gave up on Barnabas, so Barnabas didn't want to give up on other people. That included Paul.

When people were mean to the followers of Jesus, Paul held their coats and cheered them on. That was before he met Jesus. People didn't think Paul could be different on his own. They were right. But God could change Paul, and He did.

Barnabas remembered how God changed him, so he believed God had changed Paul. When no one else wanted to have anything to do with Paul, Barnabas was just the friend he needed. Barnabas even had the nickname "Son of Encouragement." Paul was grateful for his new friend.

Barnabas became Paul's coach. Paul wanted to follow Jesus, and Barnabas showed him how to do it.

Because people were afraid of Paul, Barnabas took him on a missionary trip that lasted a long time.

The two friends traveled to towns with big names like Antioch, Lystra, Derbe, and Iconium. If you thought those names were hard, there was also Pisidia, Pamphylia, Perga, and Attalia. Sharing the good news about Jesus was more important than knowing how to say the names of the cities they visited. Barnabas shared his gift of encouragement with everyone. People like to be encouraged.

Paul needed someone like Barnabas to help him learn more about Jesus. He needed someone to believe in him when no one trusted him. Paul needed Barnabas because good friends are hard to find, and Barnabas was an amazing friend.

Barnabas taught Paul, and Paul taught the people they met in each city.

"God's rescue plan is here," Paul once told a crowd. "The people who first saw Jesus didn't believe He was God's Son. They didn't like Him, and they killed Him. God knew this would happen, so He brought Jesus back to life after three days. Many people saw Him, and many now believe in Him. He brought salvation to all who believe. My friend Barnabas and I are here to share this good news. Jesus is alive, and He loves you. Accept His forgiveness and believe He has the power to rescue you."

Barnabas knew this was a message that was new to many who listened, but it was powerful because it was true.

Each day the two men walked side by side down streets, along roads, and by the sea. Each day they talked about the love of Jesus. Each day their friendship grew.

We all need friends. We all need to be encouraged. Paul had Barnabas.

It is heroic to encourage, because it is very easy to be rude. Paul had been rude to the Christians in Jerusalem, but when he became a Christian, he needed to stop. God knew that encouragement would help Paul change.

God works to make sure we can find people who will help us follow His Son, Jesus. That could be someone in our family, someone at church, or even a neighbor who really loves Jesus. Usually the person who can help us will be older and wiser. He or she may have to be really honest and tell us when we do the wrong things. This is one of the best ways we can learn.

The more time we spend with an encourager like Barnabas, the more God can use us to encourage others. This is a great thing, because people—just like you—need to be encouraged.

LEARNING FROM A HERO

Paul needed a friend. It would have been easy for Barnabas to ignore Paul, but God gave him the gift of encouragement.

1. If God had asked you to be friends with Paul, how would you have responded?
2. Why is it hard to be friends with rude people?
3. Who can you encourage today?

When you encourage others, think of their needs more than your needs. That's what God has done for you.

TIMOTHY

Story Address:
Acts 16

Heroic Quality:
Disciple

Be Heroic:
"Your love for one another will prove to
the world that you are my disciples."
JOHN 13:35

He Chose to Follow

Timothy was young and didn't have much training in the things in life that really matter. That was before he met his friend Paul.

Paul had misunderstood God's plan when he was younger and had made many wrong choices. Paul didn't want Timothy to make the same mistakes.

Timothy lived in the town of Lystra, and Paul visited whenever he could. He treated Timothy as if he were a son. He wanted to help Timothy make good choices and follow a great God.

Even when Paul was in prison, Timothy showed he was the hero of discipleship. He wanted to learn. He wanted to grow. He wanted to share God's perfect headline—JESUS LOVES TO RESCUE SINNERS.

Timothy was invited on many of Paul's mission trips. Timothy got to see some of the wonderful things Paul wrote about in his books. With each new mission trip, Timothy was learning more and becoming a champion God could use to teach others about His plans.

Paul wrote two letters to Timothy to help him as he began to lead a church of his own. Paul said, "Some people might think you can't teach because you are young. Don't listen to them. I want you to be a good example to all believers no matter how old they are. Show them who God is by how you live your life, by how you show God's love, in the way you show your faith, and in the purity of right choices."

Barnabas was a friend God used to help Paul learn how to follow Jesus. Paul was Timothy's friend. The apostle also wanted to help him learn.

Paul reminded Timothy how much his mother and grandmother loved Jesus. He made sure the young man understood that he really could follow God. Paul encouraged every good thing Timothy did.

The apostle even told Timothy in one of his letters, "God gets to hear me say thank You every day. You are part of the reason I rejoice, Timothy. I pray for you every day. I will be joyful when we can talk face-to-face again. Your faith is genuine, so keep letting God show through your life like a torch in the dark. Why? Because God doesn't want us to live in fear. He wants our lives to show His love through His power and by our choice to live lives of discipleship. Never be ashamed of God. He's the only One who can save us. He wants us to give Him our lives and our plans. My dear Timothy, this was God's plan for you from the beginning."

Timothy was a champion of learning. He understood how important it was to know what God wanted, so he went into training. He was used by God in many ways. He traveled to many places telling others about Jesus. He helped Paul write as many as six different books of the Bible.

He led the church in Ephesus. This started because Timothy was willing to be trained and Paul was willing to train.

Jesus did not want just twelve disciples. He wanted millions. Jesus wanted people to know that following Him was more than just thinking about Him from time to time. Timothy is a great example of a hero committed to learning about the most important thing we can ever know—the love of God and the plans He has for our lives. This is what it means to be a disciple.

LEARNING FROM A HERO

Timothy is a great example of discipleship because he made the choice to spend his life learning how to follow Jesus.

1. Why should you learn about Jesus?
2. How did Timothy learn to follow Jesus?
3. Why is it important to have someone help you be a disciple?

Being a disciple means you are interested in letting God teach you how to make every decision.

It All Matters to Jesus. . .

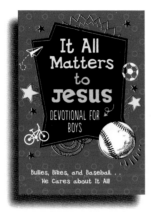

It All Matters to Jesus Devotional for Boys

Ever wonder if Jesus really cares about your new bike, your favorite app, or how you treat your little sister? Each of the 40 brief devotional chapters in *It All Matters to Jesus* offers reassurance that He does care whether or not you told a "little white lie" at school. . . how you treat Mom and Dad. . .how you spend your free time. . .your daily struggles and cares. . . He cares about every little—and BIG!—thing. Find the heavenly Father in life's daily details and come to know just how much He cares for you!

Paperback / 978-1-63058-921-9 / $5.99

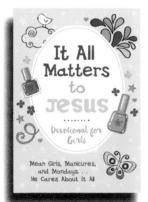

It All Matters to Jesus Devotional for Girls

Each of the 40 brief devotional chapters offers girls reassurance that it all really does matters to Jesus! How you treat your siblings. . .what you write about in your journal. . .how you treat Mom and Dad. . .how you spend your free time—painting, drawing, dancing, spending time in God's Word. . .your daily struggles and cares. . .He cares about every little—and BIG!— thing.

Paperback / 978-1-63058-933-2 / $5.99

About the Author

Glenn A. Hascall is an accomplished writer with credits in more than one hundred books, including titles from Thomas Nelson, Bethany House, and Regal. His writing has appeared in numerous publications around the globe. He's also an award-winning broadcaster, lending his voice to animation and audio drama projects.